Performance Appraisal

Concepts and Techniques for
Postsecondary Education

74437

Bettye B. Burkhalter

James A. Buford, Jr.

Performance Appraisal

Concepts and Techniques for

Postsecondary Education

Performance appraisal is conducted in all types of organizations and groups. Postsecondary educational institutions are no exception. Postsecondary administrators appraise the actions of department heads, faculty, and support personnel to measure their contribution to the objectives of the institution. Some administrators perform this task perfunctorily and fail to see its value, while others see it as a valuable process. Members of the organization must receive feedback from others concerning the appropriateness of their behavior if they are to improve productivity, correct errors, and grow professionally.

Terms used to describe this process vary among professional groups. Performance appraisal also is known as performance evaluation, merit rating, performance review, performance and productivity assessment, and efficiency and fitness reporting. Performance appraisal has become the preferred term and is used in the most recent personnel and compensation textbooks and professional literature. The term evaluation should be avoided since it refers to those processes used to establish the internal worth of jobs.

The process of performance appraisal varies from a series of informal assessments made by superiors who know their staff well to more structured systems which require superiors to complete various forms and make written comments. Many authorities contend that well-designed performance appraisal systems are essential in effectively and legally managing human resources.

In reality, however, few systems are totally successful. One reason is that superiors have great difficulty writing useful and objective performance appraisal reports. They are often reluctant to criticize a subordinate's work and put the criticism in writing. Another problem is there is no single approach that can fully address all the purposes that organizations attempt to achieve with performance appraisal. As for equal opportunity considerations, many systems used today are not the solution but, rather, are part of the problem. A number of studies have shown criterion bias to be a serious shortcoming, resulting in discrimination against blacks, ethnic minorities, and women. These systems may produce ratings that are subjective, impressionistic, non-job-related, and unstandardized. When used to justify important personnel decisions, such ratings increase rather than decrease Equal Employment Opportunity (EEO) liability.

Fortunately, the failures of the past have led to increased emphasis on development of raters, more realistic expectations of what performance appraisal can accomplish, workable appraisal techniques, and effective strategies to deal with EEO regulations. Examples of effective performance appraisal systems can be found in all types of organizations including educational institutions. Turning the potential of performance appraisal into productive reality is a challenge but attainable goal facing those who manage the affairs of postsecondary education.

With few exceptions, both faculty and administrators approach the performance appraisal process with some level of anxiety and apprehension. The editors have made a concerted effort in this book to relieve some of this anxiety by presenting the most pertinent information which will increase the understanding of basic knowledge that makes any performance appraisal system workable, fair to all parties, and legally defensible. While the editors recognize that many facets were omitted that could have been included, to do so would have made it unnecessarily long.

This book is not intended to be a substitute for primary sources in the field; rather, it is meant to provide a concise framework for understanding the basic concepts of performance appraisal and serve as a functional tool for practitioners and scholars. In addition, our book is not designed to render legal advice or legal opinion. Such advice may only be given by licensed, practicing attorney, and only when related to actual fact situations. This warning is particularly pertinent because of the nature of the topics covered herein. Specific legal questions concerning personnel performance appraisal should always be checked with the appropriate legal counsel.

Bettye B. Burkhalter
James A. Buford, Jr.

Acknowledgments

The editors and contributors wish to thank the many administrators, faculty, graduate students, and support staff who made this work possible. We particularly are indebted to the following people for their comments or editorial assistance on one or more of the chapters in this book: William H. Holley, Bettye Campbell, Hayden D. Center, and James Palmer.

Special acknowledgement goes to Anne S. Stewart who provided on-site leadership for the study which led to the development of a performance appraisal system at Southern Union State Junior College. Special acknowledgment also is given to Deborah J. Miller-Wood for research assistance and for development of additional appraisal procedures from the study.

Contents

Appendices

Performance Appraisal: An Overview

Bettye B. Burkhalter

Appraisal of performance of faculty, administrators, and support staff is an activity which has been identified as one of the most pressing issues facing higher education during the next decade. There are a number of reasons for this growing concern including financial exigency, public pressure for accountability, and the continuing need for workable approaches to reinforce the growth and development of individuals. As might be expected, this issue has generated considerable apprehension and skepticism, particularly on the part of faculty members. It is the purpose of the authors to present in uncomplicated terms the key concepts, theories, practices, and constraints in this area. The focus is experiential and practical. Emphasis is made on the application of knowledge so that administrators will gain a useful understanding of the topic and have a frame of reference to make the best possible decisions.

Problems and Issues in Performance Appraisal

Performance appraisal is widely recognized as an essential part of the management job in all types of organizations. It can provide a source of motivation to achieve organizational goals, a measure of work related contributions, and a valuable tool in the personal and professional development of individuals. Unfortunately, performance appraisal is generally regarded as one of the weakest elements in the management process. A recent survey of over 2,400 practicing managers combined with extensive review and analysis of 25 years of literature concluded that "no industry or academician has comprehensively solved the problems in performance appraisal"; in fact, "no two people completely agree on how to solve the issue."[1] The field has apparently not progressed very far since 1972 when Cohen and Brawer pointed out that ". . . we are still at the most rudimentary empirical stage [of performance appraisal]. . . ."[2]

If one accepts these conclusions, then it would seem that there must be certain inherent characteristics within the structure and processes of organizations which are contributing factors. Thomas F. Gilbert offers the following pessimistic and unflattering assessments:

- Information is frequently inadequate and misleading; managers often do not really know how well people are performing.

- Job models seldom exist to tell people precisely what important results they are supposed to accomplish, how these results are measured, and what standards of performance are expected of them.

- Behavioral conditions for performance are rarely well supplied by management to see that people have the best data, feedback, resources, procedures, incentives, and training in order to meet exemplary standards.[3]

Finally, the topic of performance appraisal is viewed at worst as a necessary evil in private industry and many organizations in the public sector. In the field of education, the reservations are much more serious, particularly in regard to post tenure appraisal of faculty. Formalized appraisal procedures are seen by many as unworkable, detrimental to collegial relationships, and a threat to academic freedom.[4]

While the authors recognize the aforementioned problems and issues, we remain optimistic. The results of the past 25 years of research and observations of organizational practice do not support a conclusion that performance appraisal cannot be accomplished. These results simply suggest that designing and implementing a legal, accurate, and cost effective performance appraisal program is not an easy task. In fact, every organization must appraise performance because decisions must be made in such vital areas as tenure, promotion, and merit pay adjustments which require the measurement of work contributions.

Evolving Purposes of Performance Appraisal

A comprehensive performance appraisal system should provide the framework to make both administrative and professional decisions. Michael Scriven's "formative-summative" evaluation concept is widely recognized and accepted.[5] Theoretically, data from the formative dimension of performance appraisal can be used for professional development decisions, and data from the summative side can be used for personnel management decisions.[6] Many educators, researchers, and practicing professionals, however, continue to voice the concern that one appraisal system cannot serve both purposes.[7,8] Wilkinson contends that attempts to construct a single comprehensive system which serves both formative-summative functions would be an impossible task.[9] Conversely, according to the research team of Darling-Hammond, Wise, and Pease, the approaches are not mutually exclusive if the performance appraisal yields, on the one hand, objective, standardized information for accountability and, on the other, descriptive information for individual staff development.[10]

Although there is disagreement among some of the authorities in the field regarding the dual use of a formative-summative evaluation approach, as applied to a performance appraisal system, the controversy surrounding the supposed incompatibility between formative and summative purposes of appraisal is confined largely to educational research and writing. The issue does not receive a great deal of attention in management literature, nor is it viewed to be a major problem in many organizations. Therefore, the authors hold to the view that a single approach, when carefully designed and properly implemented, can serve a variety of purposes.

Professional Development

Many authorities consider professional development to be a very important aspect of performance appraisal. Research has led to the following conclusions:

- Individuals arc very interested in knowing more about the factors affecting their performance and their careers.

- Administrators are reluctant to discuss these issues.

- Most administrators have not found a direct approach to professional development issues.[11]

Using the results of performance appraisal in career development can help individuals in identifying and overcoming blocks to their progress and in developing strategies for improvement as they move through various stages of their career. This could be diagnostic; for example, statistically analyzing the links between performance ratings and career stages. Ratings can also be used directly to help staff members understand what they must do to become or remain high performers.[12]

Placement in the Organization

There are several types of placement decisions in which performance ratings may be used. The first deals with an individual's advancement in the organizational structure. Examples include faculty member to department chair, library technician to assistant librarian, and comptroller to business manager. Job behavior and activities are often more revealing than tests and interviews for predicting future performance. Thus, positive performance ratings often are used as promotion criteria. It is unrealistic to assume that because individuals are performing well on a job that they will succeed at the next higher level, particularly when they are considered for promotion from lower to upper level positions. Deliberations over which candidates will be chosen for promotions always should begin by matching the requirements of the job with the applicant's qualifications. It is possible to identify certain aspects of performance on a present job that can be useful in predicting performance in a different assignment. For example, if a faculty member received good ratings in chairing faculty committees, this would be a major consideration in a possible promotion to department head. On the other hand, a faculty member who had difficulty with daily administrative details would be a poor prospect for an administrative assignment.

The second type of placement deals with the professional, rather than administrative hierarchy. The most pervasive example is found in the faculty. Decisions must be made regarding the awarding of tenure and promotion in rank, and in some cases both at the same time. For example, an assistant professor could be tenured and promoted to associate professor simultaneously. These type decisions focus on different dimensions of performance; however, accurate assessment of appropriate behavior and outcomes such as teaching success and community service can still be achieved.

Placement also has a negative aspect. An individual who is performing poorly may need to be transferred into a new job in which prospects for adequate performance are feasible. Again, performance appraisal results that identify both strengths and weaknesses can provide information about the type of job that better utilizes an individual's strength. These results reduce or eliminate those areas where deficiencies exist.

There will be cases where, regardless of the best efforts of the organization, an individual is either unwilling or unable to meet reasonable expectations of job performance. In these cases, it is necessary to use the results of performance appraisal for such adverse actions as demotion, suspension, probation, or termination.

Compensation

An organization's reward system includes anything an employee values that the employer is willing to offer in exchange for the employee's contributions. One important reward is compensation. It is logical that the amount of an individual's salary increase should be related to job performance during a specific period. Many organizations base the amount of merit raises directly on performance ratings. There are three reasons to relate salary to performance. First, as a society we are committed to a sense of equity that suggests that rewards and performance should be related. Second, research in motivation shows that if compensation is to be a motivator, people must see a clear, positive correlation with performance. Third, research also shows that outstanding performers prefer to work in and remain in meritocracies.[13]

There are authorities in the field who feel that compensation decisions should not be linked to performance appraisal. The contention is that during the performance appraisal conference, the individual is most concerned with the amount of the raise and not with such important matters as productivity improvement and professional development. Therefore, an employee is likely to concentrate on how the rating will translate into dollars and to ignore all else.

While this issue cannot be resolved completely, it seems reasonable that if an organization is willing to invest the time and resources needed to develop a job-related performance appraisal system, the results should be used in the compensation program. The argument that if individuals know their pay increases are related to performance ratings, the other purposes of performance appraisal somehow will be minimized can be stated conversely. The person may feel that if ratings have no influence on salary, then the organization is not serious about performance appraisal.

The major concern with using performance appraisal results in compensation program decisions is whether or not the system actually measures employee contributions. Most of the dissatisfaction with merit pay can be traced directly to systems that produce highly subjective and frequently meaningless ratings. Such ratings have little to do with how well people fulfill their obligations to the organization.

Legal Considerations

Performance ratings, when used to justify decisions related to such areas as promotion, merit pay, and terminations, are subject to federal and state laws and regulations which prohibit discrimination based on race, color, sex, religion, national origin, age, and handicapping condition. The centerpiece of EEO Legislation is Title VII of the Civil Rights Act of 1964. Beginning with the landmark case, *Griggs v. Duke Power Company*, both the courts and the Equal Employment Opportunity Commission (EEOC) have mandated that appraisals be based on criteria which are valid or job related. While it is not impossible to prove job relatedness to the satisfaction of a compliance agency or court, certain essential steps must be followed. What is required, ". . . at a minimum, is a degree of logical argument and factual evidence, not just a subjective appeal to intuition and so-called common sense."[14]

An institution which loses a Title VII case is subject to back pay awards which can be substantial in a class action suit. In addition, courts usually allow the prevailing party to recover attorney fees. There have been cases where courts have found defendants to be personally liable for violating the rights of individuals. Finally, a court is likely to impose hiring and promotional quotas, as well as requiring the employer to revise its selection practices. Even if the employer wins, a lawsuit is very costly. Time and resources invested in research and analysis, answering interrogatories, and preparation for trial, unlike attorney fees, cannot be recovered.

The Selection of a Performance Appraisal Technique

Many performance appraisal methods and techniques are used today. As might be expected, no method can be expected to accomplish all of the objectives of the process and all have advantages and disadvantages. The selection of a method or combination of methods should be based on accommodating legal requirements; current research; proposed uses of appraisal results; institution type, climate, and mission; and organizational resources.

It is probably safe to suggest that there are a number of techniques which are both effective and legally defensible and an equally large number which should be rejected out of hand for failing on both counts. A somewhat neglected area is cost versus benefits. As will become evident, the development and administration of a performance appraisal program is expensive, and the value of post appraisal benefits such as increased motivation and better administrative decisions should be at least equal to the costs in time and resources.

Criterion Development

Regardless of the technique used to measure job performance, the adequacy of the criteria measures is a critical issue. There are various types of job performance measures which can emphasize both work output and judgmental data. Work output can be observed and tabulated such as number of important committees chaired, number of public service activities conducted, and the number of professional presentations and publications. Such measures are seen to be highly objective. In fact, one advocate of such measures in appraising performance of faculty members uses the expression "either you did it or you didn't."[15] There is little question, however, that judgmental data is unavoidable. Most jobs require information from superiors who directly and continuously observe the quality of the work. The distrust of these kinds of measures and the possibility of bias make it essential to carefully develop and scale behavioral measures.

In criterion development, job analysis serves both a legal and technical purpose. The legal role is well established in both the "Uniform Guidelines" and in a series of court decisions. A thorough and competent job analysis establishes the rational link between the content of the job and the content of the performance measure. According to Donald Schwartz, EEOC personnel research psychologist, "the absence of a job analysis is fatal to a validity study in a court challenge."[16]

In regard to the technical or professional requirements for job analysis, there are a number of acceptable methods. In selecting a method or technique, the focus should be on ensuring that the method or combination of methods representatively samples significant job tasks. Although it is highly desirable, it is not possible to specify one clear, suitable, standard means for meeting all the technical and legal considerations of a job analysis.[17] The lack of such a standard, however, should not be viewed as a major problem.

Measurement Accuracy

The final outcome of a performance appraisal program is, of course, the rating. Unfortunately, the process is not self regulating. Measurement accuracy is a serious concern; in fact, various types of rater errors can undermine the validity of the most carefully designed system. Performance appraisal programs must have the support of top administration; much more than a speech and a cover memo. At a minimum, all levels of management must take performance appraisal programs seriously.

It is also necessary to address tendencies and perceptual inaccuracies of raters. There are a number of common sources of error in performance appraisal which can be controlled with an adequate rater training program. While these problems cannot be completely eliminated, both accuracy and reliability can be brought to manageable levels.

Instrumentation

Finally, there is a need to set concepts and theories into operation so that performance appraisal can be implemented under standardized and controlled conditions. Instrumentation often does not receive adequate attention. In too many cases, the actual performance appraisal forms are either "off-the-shelf" or poorly designed. Each organization will, of course, have different requirements depending on the technique that is selected.

Concluding Comment

This discussion has raised a number of important issues regarding performance appraisal in postsecondary institutions and there are obviously many others. It should be apparent that there is no perfect solution to the problem of measuring work-related contributions to objectives. But the point is that performance appraisal is an essential part of the management job. There is real value in the process and the forces pressing for performance appraisal will only become stronger. While it is important to seek help from the literature, it is also possible to be overwhelmed with conflicting information. Too often this leads to a feeling of futility and a decision to avoid facing the issue until a unified model has appeared. This will not happen. The task of institutions is to integrate proven concepts into their own model, avoid the mistakes of others, and move forward.

Endnotes

1.   Evelyn Eichel and Henry E. Bender, *Performance Appraisal: A Study of Current Techniques*, (New York: American Management Associations, 1984), p. 9.

2.   Arthur M. Cohen and Florence B. Brawer, *Confronting Identity: The Community College Instructor*, (Englewood Cliffs, NJ: Prentice Hall, 1972), p. 186.

3.   Thomas F. Gilbert, "Analyzing Productive Performance," in *Handbook of Organizational Behavior Management*, ed. Lee W. Frederikson (New York: John Wiley and Sons, 1982), p. 127.

4.   Christine M. Licata, "Post-tenure Faculty Evaluation: Threat or Opportunity," *Executive Summary, ASHE - ERIC Higher Education Report 1*, (Washington, DC: Association for the Study of Higher Education, 1986), p. 1.

5.   Michael Scriven, "Summative Teacher Evaluation," in *Handbook of Teacher Education*, ed. Jason Millman (Beverly Hills, CA: Sage, 1981), pp. 244-271.

6.   Hans A. Andrews and William A. Marzano, "Faculty Evaluation: Stimulates Expectations of Excellence," *Community and Junior College Journal* 54 (December-January 1983-1984), pp. 35-37.

7.   Peter Seldin, "Improving Faculty Evaluation Systems," *Peabody Journal of Education* 59 (January 1982), pp. 93-99.

8.   Arthur M. Cohen, "Evaluation of Faculty," *Community College Review* 2 (Summer 1974), p. 12-21.

9.   L. Wilkerson, "Faculty Development." Paper presented at Conference of Professional and Organizational Development Network, Memphis, 1979.

10.   Linda Darling-Hammond, Arthur E. Wise, and Sara R. Pease, "Teacher Evaluation in the Organizational Context: A Review of the Literature," *Review of Educational Research* 53 (Fall 1983), pp. 285-328.

11.   Paul H. Thompson, Robin Z. Baker, and Norman Smallwood, "Improving Professional Development by Applying the Four Stage Career Model," *Organizational Dynamics* 15 (Autumn 1986), p. 50.

12.   *Ibid.*, pp. 54 and 62.

13.   Edward Lawler, "Performance Appraisal and Merit Pay," in *Creative Personnel Practices: New Ideas for Local Government*, ed. John Matzer, Jr. (Washington, DC: International City Management Association, 1984), p. 75.

14.   James Ledvinka, *Federal Regulation of Personnel and Human Resource Management*, (Boston: Kent, 1982) p. 43.

15.   James L. Smith, personal communication, March 1987. Dr. Smith is the Head of Personnel and Staff Development for the Cooperative Extension Service, Auburn University and has designed a faculty appraisal system that has withstood several court challenges.

16.   Bureau of National Affairs, "Professional, Legal Requirements of Job Analysis Explored at Chicago Conference," *Daily Labor Report*, May 30, 1980, p. A5.

17.   Robert D. Gatewood and Hubert S. Feild, *Human Resource Selection*, (Homewood, IL: Dryden, 1987), p. 176.

2

Legal Aspects of Performance Appraisal

James A. Buford, Jr.

Although most of the attention in the area of equal employment opportunity has been focused on recruitment and selection, the performance appraisal process is subject to the same laws and guidelines. Decisions related to promotion, selection for training programs, wage and salary administration, discipline, and even dismissal come from performance appraisal results. Title VII of the Civil Rights Act of 1964 prohibits employment discrimination based on race, color, religion, sex, or national origin. The Age Discrimination in Employment act of 1967 prohibits discrimination against people age 40 and over. The Equal Employment Opportunity Commission (EEOC) has been given legislative responsibility for enforcing these acts. In 1966 the EEOC issued its first set of "Guidelines" relating to the employer's obligation to develop nondiscriminatory personnel procedures. They were revised in 1970 and again in 1978.[1]

Major Court Decisions

In 1971 the U.S. Supreme Court in *Griggs v. Duke Power Company* issued a landmark decision regarding Title VII. The effect of the Court's decision was to establish a requirement that if any employment practice or "test" has an adverse impact on members of a protected group, the employer must demonstrate that the practice is valid or job-related.[2] The decision also gave the EEOC "Guidelines" essentially the force of law in developing personnel procedures. Performance appraisal results, when used to justify personnel decisions, are clearly covered by Title VII and related laws.

In 1973 the court stated in *Brito v. Zia Company* that the organization had violated Title VII when, on the basis of poor performance ratings, it laid off a number of employees.[3] The court said the practice was illegal because (1) a disproportionate number of Hispanic workers were laid off and (2) the performance appraisal instrument was not related to important elements of work behavior but was based on "the best judgments and opinions of supervisors" and was not administered and scored under controlled and standardized conditions. The decision also clearly established that performance ratings were employment "tests."

There was a similar case involving a university in 1974. In *Wade v. Mississippi Cooperative Extension Service*, a U.S. District Court noted that what the organization had called an "objective appraisal of performance" actually was based on supervisory ratings of traits such as leadership, public acceptance, attitude, grooming, personal conduct, outlook on life, resourcefulness, and loyalty.[4] The court ruled that the results of such appraisals retained black employees in nonsupervisory positions and that the results could not be used as promotion criteria. The court ordered the Extension Service to develop an appraisal system that would meet the requirements of the EEOC "Guidelines." Both of these cases are classic examples of discrimination as defined in the Griggs case.

In 1975 the U.S. Supreme Court ruled in *Albermarle v. Moody* that because job analysis had not been conducted, the company could not use performance appraisal ratings to validate selection requirements which eliminated a disproportionate number of black applicants.[5] The importance of adequate job analysis continues to be emphasized. In *Greenspan v. The Automobile Club of Michigan*, a case brought in 1980, the court criticized the method used in analyzing jobs, stating, "The analyst did not verify job description by making an on-site inspection of the employee who actually performed the job. . . ."[6] The major requirement in job analysis for performance appraisal purposes is to ensure that the data collected provides accurate information about work behaviors critical on the job.

EEO Liability

EEO laws and court decisions attempt to eliminate race, sex, or age discrimination, and liability can be triggered in at least three general ways: intent to discriminate, disparate treatment, and disparate or adverse impact.

Intent to discriminate was the major consideration in discrimination cases prior to the passage of Title VII. Persons seeking recourse had to prove that the employer deliberately set out to discriminate against them on the basis of race (there was no prohibition against sex or age discrimination). Intent to discriminate is evidenced by the following examples:

- A rater deliberately gives lower performance ratings to black employees.

- Prejudicial statements are made such as "blacks cannot handle management responsibilities."

- Policy statements endorse illegal practices such as job segregation.

At the present time, intent to discriminate is not a major factor in EEO litigation; however, evidence of such actions will discredit any defense raised by an employer.

Disparate treatment occurs when members of protected groups are treated differently from other employees. Examples of this include:

- A black and white employee receive different ratings when there is no observable difference in job performance.

- Male employees receive day-to-day counseling to improve their performance ratings. Female employees do not.

Disparate treatment is a frequent cause of discrimination complaints.   Under present law it is not necessary to provide evidence of "evil intent"; all that is required to establish the fact that a procedure or practice is not carried out consistently between individuals or groups.

Disparate impact occurs when barriers which appear to be neutral have an adverse effect on members of protected groups.   There may be no intent to discriminate or evidence that one group or individual is treated differently from another.   In many cases, statistics alone are sufficient to establish disparate impact.   The EEOC and the courts have adopted the 80 percent rule for such cases.   The rule states that any selection ratio (e.g., number promoted vs. number eligible) for members of protected groups must be at least 80 percent of the majority selection ratio.[7]   Examples include:

- A statistical analysis reveals that blacks receive significantly lower performance ratings than whites.

- Performance ratings lead to differential promotions, training opportunities, merit raises, or dismissals.

Disparate impact focuses on the effect of practices and procedures rather than the causes.   Another term that is used for disparate impact is systemic discrimination.

Intent to discriminate and disparate treatment can involve individuals or groups of people who are members of a protected class.   Disparate impact normally involves groups.   The existence of any one can start a chain of events known as the EEO liability process.[7]

Typically, an organization first learns that it has been accused of discrimination when it receives a notice of charge from the EEOC.   If there is a state fair employment practices agency, the EEOC must defer to that agency before beginning its own investigation.   The deferral agency may process and settle the charge.   If the charge is not settled, or the agency waives jurisdiction, the EEOC will re-assume jurisdiction.   The EEOC will first invite the employer to attend a "no-fault" conference to resolve the complaint.   If, in the opinion of the EEOC representative, the charge has merit, there will be an attempt to obtain a settlement.   If the charge is found to be without merit, the EEOC will issue a "no-reasonable-cause" finding.

If the representative is unable to settle a charge which is thought to have merit, the EEOC will then conduct a full-scale investigation.   The EEOC has the authority to subpoena and question witnesses under oath.   If the investigation results in a finding of "cause," the EEOC will again attempt to conciliate the matter. At this point, conciliation remedies might include back pay, promotion, changes in procedures and relief for others similarly affected. If the investigation reveals "no-reasonable-cause," the EEOC will issue a right-to-sue letter to the complainant. Faced with a finding of "cause," the organization will often elect to settle the case rather than take a chance on losing in court. If conciliation fails, the EEOC has direct access to the courts, and will consider litigation based on the merits of the case. Actually, most charges do not result in litigation but are resolved through administrative action.

If the case goes to court, the complainant (plaintiff) must, as shown earlier, prove a *prima facie* case of discrimination by showing intent to discriminate, disparate treatment, or disparate impact. This is the first burden of proof in a discrimination case and is always carried by the plaintiff.

Once the plaintiff has established a *prima facie* case in a disparate treatment claim, the employer must articulate some legitimate, non-discriminatory reason for making the decision. When disparate impact is established, the employer must show that the practice or procedure has a "manifest relationship" to the job in question. This holds even when the criteria are, by necessity, "subjective or discretionary" in nature. The employer may show that the practice is necessary to fill a legitimate business requirement. This is known as the defense of "business necessity." Another defense is to demonstrate that the practice is valid or job-related according to the "Guidelines." There are variants and combinations of these defenses, but the important point to remember is that, once a *prima facie* case has been established, the employer is presumed to have violated Title VII unless the employer can show otherwise.[8] The second burden of proof (some authorities use the term *burden of production*) in an EEO case is always carried by the employer.

If the employer's defense is successful, the plaintiff must show that the employer's reasons were, in fact, only a pretext, or that alternate selection methods having less adverse impact are available. This third burden is carried by the plaintiff. EEO cases, however, are normally decided on the basis of whether or not employers can demonstrate that their practices are job-related (see Figure 2.1).

The discussion above outlines how a charge would typically be decided in a court case. Most charges, of course, do not result in actual litigation, but are resolved by the EEOC or state agency through administrative action, either by a "no cause" finding, or, if "reasonable cause" is found, through conciliation.[9]

An employer who loses a Title VII case is subject to back pay awards (which can be substantial in a class action suit). Also, courts normally allow the prevailing party to recover attorney fees. There have been cases where courts have found defendants to be personally liable for violating the rights of individuals. Finally, a court is likely to impose hiring and promotional quotas, as well as requiring the employer to revise its practices. Even if the employer wins, a lawsuit is very costly. Time and resources

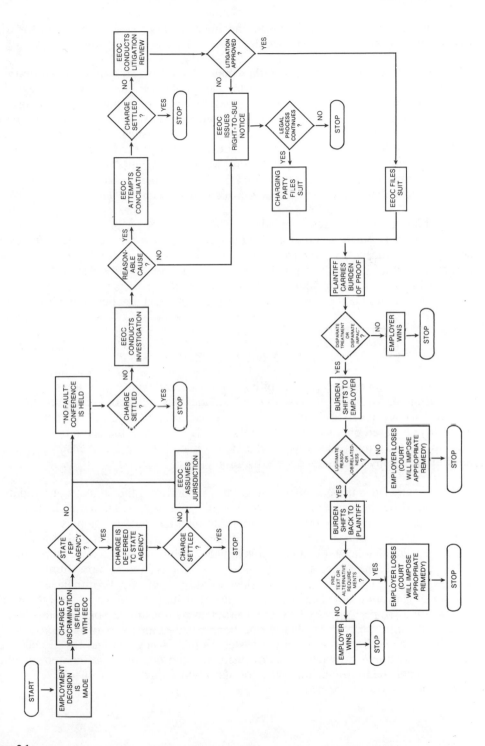

Figure 2.1

invested in research and analysis, answering interrogatories, and preparation for trial, unlike attorney fees, cannot be recovered.

There are three basic approaches that may be used by an employer to minimize EEO liability. The first is to hire, promote, and administer salaries without regard to performance. For example, promotions could be based on seniority, and across the board raises could be given. The employer could thus ensure that there would be no adverse impact, and a *prima facie* case could not be established. The second approach would be to continue current invalidated practices and wait for the EEOC or minority applicants or employees to take legal action. Many organizations follow this practice. A third approach would be to assume that performance appraisal practices will have adverse impact and validate each practice in accordance with the "Guidelines."

The third approach is recommended. The idea of being prepared to defend the organization's performance appraisal practices after a *prima facie* case has been established does not mean that adverse impact is something that should not be avoided whenever possible. One does not purchase automobile liability insurance with the intention of causing a traffic accident. In fact, insured motorists are likely to be safer drivers. It is also true that job-related performance appraisal practices have less adverse impact.

A Validation Strategy

The goal of minimizing EEO liability is realistic and well within the capability of any organization. Although no system can be made "lawsuit proof," there are measures which can reduce the possibility of systemic discrimination. The approach recommended here is based on a strategy of validation. By requiring the validation of performance appraisal systems according to the "Guidelines," this strategy ensures adequate defense if an employer is charged with discrimination.

Not all authorities in personnel management recommend the strategy of validation. One view held by the opposing group of practitioners, writers, and consultants is that validation can be done only by experts and that another strategy, namely reducing or eliminating adverse impact, is preferred. Although it is true that validation is required only where a practice is having an adverse impact, such reasoning is not compelling. In the first place, if one accepts the definition of validity, that a procedure or "test" measures what it purports to measure, then validity itself is a legitimate end. Why would an organization not take steps to ensure that its performance appraisal system was measuring job performance? Another problem with a strategy of reducing adverse impact is that this approach implicitly questions whether members of protected groups can perform adequately even when the system is fair. They can and do. Finally, the "Uniform Guidelines" provide validation methods, and one of these (content validity) can be accomplished without the need for statistical expertise. A checklist for legal requirements is shown in Appendix B.

Reducing or eliminating adverse impact and improving the utilization of protected group members in all parts of the work force is more properly an objective than a strategy. Employers who find themselves accused of Title VII violations because members of protected groups are either rejected for promotion at a disproportionate rate, underrepresented in the work force, or receive lower pay are usually unable to successfully defend in court the practices in question. An analysis of these cases strongly suggests that these employers have almost always waited until they got into trouble before they attempted to justify their practices, many of which were not job-related. These employers were, to use a common expression, "a day late and a dollar short." Thus, a strategy of validation would seem to have two major advantages. First, it addresses the problem of systemic discrimination, which Congress and the courts have identified as the major barrier to fair employment. Second, validation contributes to better administrative decisions.

The best strategy for demonstrating that a performance appraisal system is job-related is known as content validity, in which a procedure is justified by showing that it representatively samples significant parts of a job. The following excerpts from the "Uniform Guidelines" define content validity in more detail.

A selection procedure* may be supported by a content validity strategy to the extent that it is a representative sample of the content of the job.

. . . a content validity strategy is not appropriate for demonstrating the validity of selection procedures which purport to measure traits or constructs such as intelligence, aptitude, personality, common sense, judgment, leadership, and spatial ability. Content validity is also not an appropriate strategy when the selection procedure involves knowledge, skills, or abilities which an employee will be expected to learn on the job.

There should be job analysis which includes an analysis of the important work behaviors required for successful performance and their relative importance. Any job analysis should focus on work behavior(s) and the tasks associated with them.

To demonstrate the content validity of a procedure, a user should show that the behaviors demonstrated in the selection procedure provide a representative sample of the work product of the job. . . . The closer the content and the context of the selection procedure are to work samples or work behaviors, the stronger is the basis for showing content validity.[10]

---

*The term selection procedure refers to any procedure used for any employment decision; thus a performance appraisal procedure is a selection procedure within the meaning of the "Uniform Guidelines" (see Section 16Q).

Related Considerations

While the classic defense against adverse impact is for the employer to show job-relatedness, the situation is not so simple with performance appraisal. Since it is difficult or impossible to develop a completely objective system, there always will be elements of supervisory judgment. Courts have varied their criteria for finding discrimination. Factors which are considered include: the facts in the case; the degree of adverse impact; if the criteria are objective, subjective, or some combination; and whether or not the practice operates to perpetuate the effects of earlier intentional discrimination.[11]   Thus, extreme care should be taken in the choice of measures, standardization and control of ratings, training of raters, and analysis of results to ensure that ratings are not biased by (age) race, color, sex, national origin, or religion.[12]

Two recent studies examined empirically the effects of 13 appraisal system characteristics on the verdicts in 66 federal court cases involving charges of discrimination.   Five characteristics were found to correlate strongly with judgments for the defendants.[13]

1.   Type of Organization - Public sector organizations were more likely to receive a favorable verdict than private businesses.

2.   Provision of Written Instructions - Many courts have held the view that the provision of written instructions, while no guarantee, is a prerequisite for systematic, unbiased appraisals.

3.   Traits vs. Behavioral-Oriented Appraisals - Courts are far more likely to accept behaviorally-based performance appraisal systems.

4.   Use of Job Analysis - Defendants have won approximately 82 percent of the time when the system was based on job analysis.

5.   Review of Appraisal Results - Defendants were more successful when results of the appraisal were discussed with the employee.

"At Will" Liability

Beginning with the industrial revolution, the employee-employer relationship in the United States has been covered by the common law doctrine of "employment-at-will." Under this doctrine, either the employer or employee can terminate the relationship at any time and without giving reason.

The doctrine clearly favors the employer, since it contains the right to arbitrarily dismiss an employee. Increasingly, however, this right has become subject to both statutory and judicial restrictions. As has been pointed out, the effect of federal EEO laws has become a major constraint. In recent years, however, both federal and state courts have created new legal rights for employees including those who are not members of protected groups (women, minorities, persons over 40, etc.). In regard to performance appraisal, employers may encounter legal liability when they attempt to discharge employees for poor performance. Two important sources of at-will liability involving performance appraisal are breach of contract and violation of the implied convenant of "good faith and fair dealing."[14]

There have been a number of successful lawsuits where the employer has been charged with breach of contract. Representation made in employee handbooks, policies, procedures, and direct or indirect statements are implied contracts. Once a contract has been found to exist, either in fact or by implication, the employee has a legal claim if its terms are not followed. The common claim of breach of contract is when employers fail to follow their own specified procedures when discharging employees for poor performance.[15]

Courts are also allowing wrongful discharge suits where termination constitutes a violation of the implied convenant of "good faith and fair dealing." Arbitrary and unexplained firings are often overturned, and courts are making it clear that employees are entitled to varying amounts of organizational due process.[16] Employees of public institutions have additional due process rights guaranteed by the 14th Amendment to the U.S. Constitution. In other words, an employee who is being dismissed or pressured to resign (constructively discharged) for poor performance should have an opportunity to defend his or her performance and be judged in a fair way with explicit knowledge of the criteria on which the dismissal was based.

Closing Remarks

Disparate impact is a major issue in all personnel procedures. It is unrealistic to assume that performance appraisal systems can be designed which will never cause disparate impact or can be made court-proof by establishing business necessity or job relatedness. Moreover, the area of at-will liability is still evolving. But it has been demonstrated that a performance appraisal system that avoids court problems encountered by other organizations, that meets the validity requirements of the "Uniform Guidelines," and that is administered by trained raters under standardized and controlled conditions will greatly reduce the potential for legal liability.

Endnotes

1. "Uniform Guidelines on Employee Selection Procedures," *Federal Register* 43 (August 25, 1978), pp. 38290-40223. These were referred to in earlier editions (1966 and 1970) as "EEOC Guidelines."

2. *Griggs v. Duke Power Company*, 401, U.S. 430 (1971).

3. *Brito v. Zia Company*, 478 F. 2D. 1200 (1973).

4. *Wade v. Mississippi Cooperative Extension Service*, 372F. supp. 126, 7EPD 9186 (1974).

5.   *Albermarle Paper Company v. Moody*, U.S. Supreme Court Nos. 74-389 and 74-428, 10 FEP cases 1181 (1975).

6.   *Greenspan v. Automobile Club of Michigan*, 22 FEP, 195 (1980).

7.   "Uniform Guidelines," *op. cit.*, p. 38302.

8.   For examples of evidentiary burdens, see *McDonnell Douglas Corp. v. Green*, 411 U.S. 792 (1973), *Texas Dept. of Community Affairs v. Burdine* 450 U.S. 248 (1981), and *Watson v. Fort Worth Bank & Trust*, U.S. Supreme Court No. 86-6139 (1988).

9.   This discussion of the EEO liability process is taken from Kenneth J. McCulloch, *Selecting Employees Safely Under the Law*, (Englewood Cliffs, NJ: Prentice-Hall, 1981), pp. 165-242.

10.   "Uniform Guidelines," *op. cit.*, p. 38302.

11.   *Watson v. Fort Worth Bank & Trust*, U.S. Supreme Court No. 86-6139 (1988).

12.   J. Vernon Odom, "Performance Appraisal: Legal Aspects," in *The Performance Appraisal Sourcebook*, eds. Lloyd S. Baird, Richard W. Beatty, and Craig Eric Schneier (Amherst, MA: Human Resource Development Press, 1982), p. 112.

13.   Hubert S. Feild and William H. Holley, "The Relationship of Performance Appraisal Characteristics to Verdicts in Selected Employment Discrimination Cases," *Academy of Management Journal* 25 (June 1982), pp. 392-406; and H. S. Feild and D. T. Thompson, "Study of Court Decisions in Cases Involving Employee Performance Appraisal Systems," *Bureau of National Affairs, Daily Labor Report*, December 26, 1984, pp. E1-E5.

14.   A comprehensive analysis of these and other issues including court cases is found in David M. Mackey, *Employment at Will and Employer Liability* (New York: American Management Association, 1986), see especially pp. 44-47, 55-58, and 61-66.

15.   For example, see *Weiner v. McGraw-Hill, Inc.*, N.Y. Ct. App. (1982).

16.   *Board of Regents v. Roth*, 408 U.S., 564 (1972). See also *Cleveland Board of Education v. Loudermill* 470 U.S. 532 (1985), and *Yates v. Board of Regents of Lamar University System*, 654 F. Supp. 979 (E.D. Tex., 1987).

3

Considerations in Selecting a Performance Appraisal Technique

James A. Buford, Jr.

Performance appraisal systems are built around a number of methods and techniques. In selecting a technique (or combination of techniques) the institution should consider the following:

1. Does the technique accurately measure job performance?

2. Does it meet legal requirements?

3. Who will perform the appraisal function?

4. Can it be administered efficiently?

5. Are the post-appraisal benefits in the areas of productivity, motivation, and decision-making likely to exceed the costs?

To provide a basis for answering these questions, we will explain the characteristics of a number of performance appraisal methods and techniques, the various sources of appraisal data, and conclude with an approach to the question of costs vs. benefits.

Overview of Performance Appraisal Techniques

Many performance appraisal methods and techniques are used today. No method alone can be expected to accomplish all objectives of the performance appraisal process, and all have advantages and disadvantages. The methods described in this section are those that are most common. They include graphic rating scales, essay appraisals, comparative methods, checklist methods, critical incidents, performance standards, behavioral scales, and management by objectives.

Graphic Rating Scales

Introduced in 1922, the graphic rating scale is the oldest and most commonly used performance appraisal technique.[1]   An example is provided in Figure 3.1.   In this method, a scale is used to rate the individual on several factors.   The rater scores each factor on a continuum from low to high.

Graphic rating scales vary in two important ways, both having a major impact on reliability and validity.

The first way that graphic rating scales vary involves the factors to be rated.   These may be a list of traits such as leadership ability, initiative, honesty, and attitude.   The problem with these factors is that they are highly subjective and may not apply to the job.   For example, it is difficult to define and measure a trait such as leadership ability.   Moreover, this trait will not always be relevant, as in the case of a bookkeeper.   In most cases, trait-based scales will not meet validity requirements of the EEOC and the courts when used to justify decisions regarding promotion, merit increases, and dismissal.[2]

Figure 3.2 is a rating scale format that has been dimensionalized and weighted.   These factors are based on job domains or major responsibilities and the relative importance of each as established by job analysis.   When used with an accurate job description, this format is very job-related.   In a more detailed version of the dimensionalized rating scale format, the factors to be rated describe actual job behaviors and are known as performance standards.   An example is shown in Appendix A.   In general, the more factors there are that are job-specific and can be either quantitatively measured or at least observed, the higher the degree of reliability and validity that can be obtained.

The second way that graphic rating scales vary is the manner in which total scores are assigned.   In many cases, ratings are simply added together; however, the additivity assumption may not be valid because the factors are not equal in importance.

Ratings are more meaningful when they are weighted in accordance with their importance to overall job performance.   With quality job analysis, it is possible to develop rating scales that are weighted on an appropriate basis such as amount of time spent, frequency of performance, or relative importance.   For example, the factor used to rate instruction probably would receive a greater weight than community service, even when both are part of the job.   About 75 percent of graphic rating scales used today are similar to the one shown in Figure 3.1.   They are unweighted and are focused on traits rather than job-related behaviors.[3]

In isolation, a trait-oriented scale is of little use in providing feedback to individuals for improvement.   However, graphic rating scales are relatively simple to develop, easy to understand, and less time-consuming to administer than other techniques.   They

EMPLOYEE RATING FORM

Name _____ Classification _____

Department _____ Date _____

PERFORMANCE FACTORS	RATING				
	Poor 1	Fair 2	Average 3	Good 4	Excellent 5
1. Knowledge	☐	☐	☐	☐	☐
2. Initiative	☐	☐	☐	☐	☐
3. Cooperation	☐	☐	☐	☐	☐
4. Dependability	☐	☐	☐	☐	☐
5. Adaptability	☐	☐	☐	☐	☐
6. Attitude	☐	☐	☐	☐	☐
7. Judgement	☐	☐	☐	☐	☐
8. Creativity	☐	☐	☐	☐	☐
9. Leadership	☐	☐	☐	☐	☐
10. Punctuality	☐	☐	☐	☐	☐

COMMENTS: _____

_____

_____

_____

_____   _____

Employee Signature   Date   Supervisor Signature   Date

Figure 3.1 Graphic Trait Rating Scale

PERFORMANCE APPRAISAL FORM

PART I   IDENTIFICATION

Name __Richard W. Martin__

Position __Faculty Member__

Rating Period From __10-1-86__ To __9-31-87__

Rater Name __Douglas Brown__

Rater Title __Department Chair__

Department __Social Science__

Date Employed __9-1-80__

Rating Scale Key

1 Fails to Meet Job Requirements
2 Essentially Meets Job Requirements
3 Fully Meets Job Requirements
4 Meets Job Requirements with Distinction
5 Exceeds Job Requirements

PART II   RATING SCALES FOR MAJOR RESPONSIBILITIES

	1	2	3	4	5
A. Instructional Planning and Preparation PCT. 10% RATING:	☐	☐	☐	☐	☐

Developing and maintaining course outlines, selecting instructional aids, and preparing classroom presentations.

COMMENTS

	1	2	3	4	5
B. Instruction PCT. 50% RATING:	☐	☐	☐	☐	☐

Teaching classes as scheduled, presenting material, information, and skills to be learned; and providing for student evaluation of instruction.

COMMENTS

	1	2	3	4	5
C. Testing and Evaluation PCT. 10% RATING:	☐	☐	☐	☐	☐

Developing and administering appropriate assessment procedures for determining student achievement; providing feedback to students, and determining final course grades.

COMMENTS

	1	2	3	4	5
D. Student Affairs PCT. 10% RATING:	☐	☐	☐	☐	☐

Assisting students in curriculum planning, sponsoring student clubs and participating in campus activities; and providing assistance with job placement.

COMMENTS

	1	2	3	4	5
E. Administration PCT. 10% RATING:	☐	☐	☐	☐	☐

Maintaining office hours, attending meetings and carrying out committee assignments; following appropriate procedures and policies for submitting reports, requesting supplies and equipment, and fulfilling other duties or assignments.

COMMENTS

	1	2	3	4	5
F. Professional Development PCT. 5 % RATING:	☐	☐	☐	☐	☐

Pursuing personal professional improvement program; participating in programs, workshops, and classes to maintain credentials and competencies.

COMMENTS

	1	2	3	4	5
G. Community Service PCT. 5 % RATING:	☐	☐	☐	☐	☐

Serving as a resource person and providing advisory services within assigned subject matter area, and contributing to welfare of community through participation in areas of interest.

COMMENTS

Figure 3.2. Dimensionalized Rating Scale

can be highly job-related and can be combined with other methods such as behaviorally-phrased essays. To make ratings more meaningful, the rater, along with completing the scale, may be asked or required to justify the rating and to discuss suggestions for improvement in space provided for written comments.

Essay Appraisals

The narrative essay is a description of the individual's job performance in the rater's own words. Often, guidelines are provided. For example, the rater may be asked to describe such things as strengths, weaknesses, and potential and to make suggestions for improvement (see Figure 3.3). The essay approach to performance appraisal assumes that a candid statement from a knowledgeable supervisor about an individual's job performance is just as valid as more formal and quantitative methods.[4]

Narrative essays can provide detailed feedback regarding job performance, particularly if the rater uses an accurate job description to ensure that all areas are covered. Most essay appraisals, however, are unstructured and vary in length and content. Another problem with essay appraisals is that the individual's rating may depend more on the writing skills of the superior than on the individual's performance.[5] Finally, this method is highly subjective, time-consuming, difficult to administer, and impractical for large groups.[6] Most authorities agree that the essay is best used as a supplement to a more structured method such as the graphic rating scale.

Comparative Methods

Comparative methods compare individuals against each other rather than against standards. Individuals may be compared on measures relating to overall job performance or on several traits or work characteristics. All comparative methods assume that job performance is distributed along a continuum from poor to outstanding. This idea is popular in the military and in the corporate world, where one hears such terms as "top five percenter" and "fast track." The results of these methods produce a listing of individuals from first to last in order of performance. Figure 3.4 illustrates how ranking involves placing individuals in order of overall performance, normally by first selecting the best and worst performers, then designating next best, and continuing until all individuals have been ranked. Figure 3.5 shows how paired comparison requires that individuals be compared one at a time with every other individual, with the final task rank determined by the number of times an individual was rated better than the other individual. In the forced distribution method, the rater assigns a specific proportion of individuals to predetermined performance categories, as shown in Figure 3.6.

The most elaborate of the comparative methods is founded on the principle of the normal distribution and is analogous to grading on the curve, in which there are a few A's and F's, slightly more B's and D's, and a large number of C's. That there is some proportion of outstanding, good, fair, and poor performers in a department or organization, however, is an unrealistic assumption.[7]

Make a clear and concise statement describing the employee's performance on each of the factors below.

Productivity: Volume of work and major accomplishments.

_____

_____

_____

_____

_____

_____

Accuracy: Meeting quality standards.

_____

_____

_____

_____

_____

_____

Coordination: Planning and organizing work and supervising employees.

_____

_____

_____

_____

_____

_____

_____

Figure 3.3. Essay Appraisal Format

Cooperation: Working relationships with others.

_____

_____

_____

_____

_____

_____

_____

Know-how: Possession of job-related knowledges and skills.

_____

_____

_____

_____

_____

_____

_____

Development: Personal strengths and areas needing improvement.

_____

_____

_____

_____

_____

_____

_____

Figure 3.3. Essay Appraisal Format (Continued)

Consider the employees in your department in terms of overall job performance. Select the best employee and put his/her name in column A, line 1. Then select the worst employee and put his/her name in column B, line 20. Continue this process until the names of all employees have been placed on the scale.

Column A (Best)

1. Warren Clark
2. Sam Burton
3. James Strawn
4. Deborah Stinson
5. William Buford
6. _____
7. _____
8. _____
9. _____
10. _____

Column B (Worst)

11. _____
12. _____
13. _____
14. _____
15. _____
16. Wilson Fowler
17. Sylvia Watt
18. Harry Larkin
19. Robert Lee
20. John McCord

Figure 3.4. Ranking Scale Using Alternative Ranking Method

Source: Adapted from Dale Yoder, *Personnel Management and Industrial Relations* (Englewood Cliffs: Prentice . Hall, 1970) p. 237.

Persons Rated	As compared to:										SCORE	RANK
	SB	WB	WC	WF	HL	RL	JM	DS	JS	SW		
Sam Burton		X		X	X	X	X	X	X	X	8	2
William Buford				X	X	X	X			X	5	5
Warren Clark	X	X		X	X	X	X	X	X	X	9	1
William Fowler					X	X	X			X	4	6
Harry Larkin						X	X				2	8
Robert Lee							X				1	9
John McCord											0	10
Deborah Stinson		X		X	X	X	X			X	6	4
James Strawn		X		X	X	X	X	X		X	7	3
Sylvia Watt					X	X	X				3	7

Note: X means that the person's performance is better than the person with whom he/she was paired. For example, Clark's performance is better than any of the others. Lee's is only better than McCord's.

Figure 3.5. Ranking With Paired Comparison

Instructions: Assign the employees in your department to the appropriate categories using the following distribution as a guide:

Outstanding (10%)	Above Average (20%)	Average (40%)	Below Average (20%)	Un-Satisfactory (10%)
W. Clark	S. Burton	D. Stinson	H. Larkin	J. McCord
	J. Strawn	W. Buford	R. Lee	
		W. Fowler		
		S. Watt		

Figure 3.6. Forced Distribution

Another problem with all comparative methods is that individuals are usually compared in terms of overall job performance. This kind of comparison limits the usefulness of the appraisal for providing feedback to the individual regarding aspects of job performance which are acceptable and those which need improvement.[8] Therefore, the results of comparative methods are likely to be meaningless and may be damaging to morale since someone must be last. To illustrate how ranking methods distort reality, consider that there is a slowest runner on the U.S. Olympic gold medal 4 x 100 relay team and a fastest runner among 45 to 55 year old finishers in a local "fun run." Comparative methods are not job-related and thus are difficult to validate.

One point can be made in defense of comparative methods. An organization may need to determine rankings for administrative purposes, such as a validity check on another method. A supervisor who has rated 10 individuals on a graphic rating scale may be asked later to list the individuals from first to last in order of performance. A strong positive rank correlation would be expected.

Checklist Methods

A checklist method known as forced choice was developed by the U.S. Army during World War II to overcome the problem of lenient performance ratings. Although there are a number of variations, the procedure usually requires raters to select from a group of statements those that are related to the individual's behavior. A group of statements is shown in Figure 3.7.

From each group of statements below, mark M beside the statement which is most descriptive of the employee's behavior and mark L beside the statement which is least descriptive.

A. _____ Inclined to avoid responsibility.

_____ Takes pride in the job.

_____ Shows poor leadership.

_____ Open to suggestions.

B. _____ Exercises good judgement.

_____ Tends to resist change.

_____ Treats subordinates with respect.

_____ Has gaps in job knowledge.

C. _____ Fails to establish priorities.

_____ Complies with policies and procedures.

_____ Pays attention to details.

_____ Does not meet deadlines.

Figure 3.7. Forced Choice Appraisal

The rater is required to pick one statement that is most descriptive and one that is least descriptive of the individual. The statements are designed so that only one of the favorable and one of the unfavorable statements is associated with job performance. This information is not provided to the rater; thus, the results of the rating are known only to the personnel department, which has the key. This kind of rating tends to be resented by both managers and individuals, and feedback is obviously impossible. There are also serious questions as to whether it is possible to develop a set of statements that distinguish between good and poor performers.

Critical Incidents

Critical incidents are reports made by knowledgeable observers of action taken by individuals who were especially effective or ineffective in accomplishing their jobs. The critical incident technique, or CIT, was developed in 1954 by John C. Flanagan.[9] Critical incidents are recorded by superiors as they happen, thus are short and to the point, and they normally consist of a single sentence. The following are examples of critical incidents that illustrate effective performance:

- Conducted formal review sessions outside regular class hours; scheduled sessions so that maximum number of students could attend (Instructor).

- Developed reading list of materials contained in library to support course objectives; keyed material to textbook (Instructor).

- Prepared for and conducted class when instructor was hospitalized unexpectedly. Covered all scheduled material for 2-week period (Division Chair).

Critical incidents also describe ineffective or poor performance such as the following:

- Was absent from scheduled class without legitimate reason and with no notice to students (Instructor).

- Made several errors in computing students' final grades, resulting in complaints to Dean and reissuing of grade reports by registrar (Instructor).

- Failed to hold performance appraisal conference with faculty member (Division Chair).

Critical incidents provide useful information, particularly when they are collected and placed in appropriate categories. For example, an instructor whose critical incidents reveal a pattern of innovation, such as developing a reading list, might be considered for a promotion to a position where this characteristic could be utilized more fully. The main disadvantages of the critical incident technique is that it is time-consuming and burdensome and it may be neglected by supervisors.[10]

Performance Standards

Performance standards require a list of conditions that will exist when a job is being performed well. Many organizations have implied performance standards, but these are not spelled out in accordance with job duties. In a formal system using performance standards, a job analysis is conducted that results in a job description setting forth what is to be done. Performance standards describe how much is expected or how well the duties are to be performed. Figure 3.8 provides an example of performance standards for an instructional position, in the dimension of "Instruction":

1. **Schedule and Attendance**. Meets classes as scheduled. Encourages attendance throughout the quarter. Records daily attendance. Meets classes for full time period. Is cooperative regarding teaching assignments.

2. **Method of Instruction**. Varies method of presentation to increase student interest. Uses class time on subject matter. Encourages student participation. Demonstrates overall knowledge of subject and presents material so that it is understood by students. Encourages students to seek help after class if needed.

3. **Presentation of Instruction**. Presents information fluently and precisely and stimulates students' interest. Attempts to make instruction a pleasant experience for students.

4. **Student Evaluation**. Administers student evaluations according to established procedures. Reviews results and uses feedback to improve teaching.

Figure 3.8. Performance Standards for Instructional Position

Standards should be established through negotiations between the individual or group of subordinates and the superior. Advocates of performance standards recommend that they be written in quantitative terms when possible. However, as the examples show, some job aspects are difficult to reduce to quantitative terms; therefore, behavioral statements must be made.

The advantages and disadvantages of the performance standards approach are as follows:[11]

The participative approach gives both the subordinate and the superior a means of sharing thoughts about work priorities and expected results. This approach tends to earn the subordinate's commitment to achieve standards and the superior's commitment to provide support and resources. The subordinate is not surprised by the appraisal results; standards are known all along so the subordinate can identify any variances as they develop and correct the problem before the formal appraisal. Appraisals and feedback interviews are more objective and less contentious because they are based on specified outcomes in the principal job segments rather than on personality traits.

The principal disadvantage of the performance standards approach is the amount of time and thought required to discuss job priorities and develop standards for all the significant segments of each job. It takes effort to agree on performance standards and define them in clear and measurable terms. Although time is difficult to schedule, it is time well spent. This process requires administrators to identify, describe, and weigh the various job objectives and results.

Behavioral Scales

The behaviorally-based instrument most frequently recommended by industrial psychologists is the behaviorally anchored rating scale (BARS). This scale was originally referred to in the literature as the behavioral expectation scale (BES), and the two terms are used interchangeably.[12]

The construction of BARS generally follows procedures developed by Smith and Kendall.[13] The first step is to collect critical incidents that describe a wide range of behavior and place them in broad categories (e.g., planning, testing and evaluation, instruction, etc.). Each category serves as one performance dimension for appraising an individual. A group of people with knowledge of the job are given the set of critical incidents and categories. Members of the group are asked to match each incident to the category they believe the incident illustrates. This procedure is known as retranslation. Incidents that are not assigned to the same category by a high percentage of the group and those that fall frequently into two or more categories are discarded. Another group of people also familiar with the job are given the final categorized list of incidents and are asked to rate each incident on a five to nine point scale, representing a continuum of job performance from outstanding to poor. The only items retained are those on which there is much agreement. These incidents are used as anchors on the rating scale, hence the term behaviorally anchored. The value given to each incident is the mean value assigned by the group. An example of BARS for the position of instructor is shown in Figure 3.9.

5.00---Professor can be expected to vary syllabus of class to fit students' background. Emphasis would be placed on projects and discussion rather than lecture. Grading is based on quality of projects and tests.

4.00---Professor can be expected to meet all classes, to add the lecture with current materials, to answer course material throughly, and present a variety of test methods

3.00---Professor can be expected to meet all classes, then deliver organized lectures with appropriate standardized testing devices.

2.00---Professor can be expected to meet almost all classes and to closely repeat text, paying little attention to outside material or student questions.

1.00---Professor can be expected to hold classes irregularly. Also can be expected to present "true life" examples frequently which have little relationship to course material.

Figure 3.9. A Behaviorally Anchored Rating Scale for the Dimension "Classroom Teaching Performance"

Source: Robert D. Gatewood and Hubert S. Feild, *Human Resource Selection*, (New York: Dryden Press, 1987), p. 505.

While BARS is highly job-related, there are several limitations. The most obvious problem is that the rater may not be able to match observed behaviors with the scale anchors.[14] There are obviously many more critical incidents which describe performance under the domain of "Classroom Teaching Performance" than the five items which are provided on the scale. Another problem is that the rater might observe both "good" and "bad" performance on the same dimension. For example, the faculty member might meet all classes, but during the same period present "true life" examples in class which frequently have little relationship to course material.

A procedure which overcomes these and other limitations of BARS is called behavioral observation scales (BOS) as set forth by Latham and Wexley.[15] The primary difference is that BOS is developed by attaching a 5-point Likert scale to identify each behavioral item as shown in Figure 3.10 for the job dimension of "Instruction":

Begins class on time						
Almost Never	1	2	3	4	5	Almost Always
Follows lesson plan						
Almost Never	1	2	3	4	5	Almost Always
Uses class time on subject matter						
Almost Never	1	2	3	4	5	Almost Always
Encourages student participation						
Almost Never	1	2	3	4	5	Almost Always
Provides outlines, handouts, and bibliographies to students						
Almost Never	1	2	3	4	5	Almost Always
Emphasizes topics of major importance						
Almost Never	1	2	3	4	5	Almost Always
Summarizes presentation						
Almost Never	1	2	3	4	5	Almost Always
Provides time for student questions						
Almost Never	1	2	3	4	5	Almost Always

Figure 3.10. Behavioral Observation Scales for the Job Dimension of "Instruction"

The major advantage of BOS is that raters are forced to make a more complete appraisal of the individual's performance, rather than emphasizing only those items which they can recall at the time of the rating and are able to match with one of the scale anchors.

A final type of behavioral scale, which is less rigorous than BARS or BOS, is an expansion of the performance standards approach. This type of scale attempts to answer such questions as "How good is exceptional?" or "How bad is unsatisfactory?" The scale is constructed by considering task statements developed by job analysis and writing statements which describe levels of performance in each job dimension. The number of levels of performance depends on the number of scale points. The underlying assumption is that for each job dimension, all tasks in the dimension will be performed in the same general way. The rater selects the description which "best fits." An example of this approach for the dimension of instructional preparation is shown in Figure 3.11.

Behaviorally based scales have several general advantages over other methods. Superiors and subordinates usually are involved in their development. The feedback provided is highly job-related, and performance appraisal sessions focus on behavior that contributes to successful job performance. There are disadvantages to these methods. BARS in particular is extremely complex, requires sophisticated statistical analysis, and is time-consuming. The development procedures for these appraisal instruments must be repeated for each job, which may not be cost-effective for those organizations that have a wide variety of jobs and have only a few individuals in each category.

Management by Objectives

Although the comparison of results achieved against plans has always been used by managers, Management by Objectives (MBO) was first proposed by Peter Drucker in 1954.[16] As a formal performance appraisal system, MBO consists of the following steps:[17]

1. Organizational goals are established during the planning process and commitment to these goals is established at all managerial levels.

2. The key results areas of the job are identified. These are highly selective areas in which the subordinate must achieve an acceptable level of performance to be successful.

3. The superior and subordinate mutually agree on several objectives within key results areas that coincide with or support organizational or departmental goals. Performance requirements and timetables are established and the subordinate is allocated the necessary resources.

METHOD OF INSTRUCTION - Presenting letters, demonstration, or laboratory supervision; using appropriate method of instruction and resources, providing out-of-class assistance when necessary.

EXCEPTIONAL   5
Uses a variety of methods, aids, and/or resource people as part of presentation, encouraging student involvement. Demonstrates comprehensive and in-depth knowledge in subject area. Stimulates and maintains student interest. Exhibits openness to ideas of students. Is enthusiastic about subject, students, and teaching.

VERY GOOD   4
Uses a variety of methods and aids to increase students' interest. Exhibits substantial knowledge in subject area. Provides outlines, handouts, and bibliographies to aid learning. Involves students in presentation. Wisely uses class time. Directly offers outside help to specific students determined to need it.

ACCEPTABLE   3
Varies method of presentation to increase student interest. Uses class time on subject matter. Encourages student participation. Demonstrates overall knowledge of subject and presents material so that it is understood by student. Encourages students to seek help after class if needed.

MARGINAL   2
Presents essential information. May use same method of presentation daily. Demonstrates basic knowledge in subject area. Answers student questions, but does not involve them in presentation. Is available for outside help when needed.

UNACCEPTABLE   1
Uses class time poorly—strays from subject. Is not available for help outside class. Does not demonstrate adequate knowledge in subject area. Does not encourage student participation.

Figure 3.11. Example of a behavioral scale based on expanding the performance standard for "Method of Instruction." The scale is not behaviorally anchored.

4. The superior and subordinate hold interim progress reviews. These reviews provide feedback to the subordinate and may involve corrective action needed to stay on target or revisions of objectives in the face of unforeseen problems.

5. At the end of the period, actual accomplishments are measured against performance requirements, and objectives for the next period are established.

For MBO to be effective, a distinction must be made between objectives in and performance requirements. Unless this distinction is made there probably will be no basis for determining if the objective was accomplished. Figure 3.12 illustrates this point:

Position	Objective	Requirements
Instructor	Improve testing and evaluation procedures	Submit list of 20 questions for departmental examination by May 1
Division Chair	Develop writing skills of freshman students	Establish and staff a writing skills laboratory
Dean	Project positive image of college to community	Present program to five civic clubs during year

Figure 3.12. Objectives and Performance Requirements

MBO has many attractive features and is especially appropriate for management positions. Performance appraisals are job-related because the objectives define the most important aspects of job performance. Where factors are subjective, the personality of a manager or subordinate may influence judgments. In some cases the superior may have difficulty explaining to the subordinate a discrepancy between objectives previously agreed upon and results attained. Should this happen, discussions must be held by the two parties until a mutual understanding is reached. These discussions can focus on problems, ways to improve, and assistance needed.

Like other appraisal systems, MBO has its disadvantages. Emphasis is placed primarily on tangible results that are easily measured. Consequently, there is often a failure to appraise important aspects of the job that cannot be explained or measured in quantitative terms. Even when such measures can be obtained, an individual's performance usually is affected by factors beyond his/her control. The exclusive use of MBO can hinder cooperation by encouraging a result-at-all-costs mentality that decreases the overall productivity of the organization.[18] Finally, performance outcomes alone do not tell individuals what they need to do to maintain or increase productivity. For example, telling the Division Chair that the writing skills laboratory is not in operation will not come as a surprise. He/she needs to know what must be done to achieve the desired result and how the organization can help. Possibly budget cutbacks have resulted in insufficient funds to hire lab instructors, or sufficient space has not been made available. Problems such as these are why many authorities emphasize the need to combine MBO with other measures of job behavior.[19]

Sources of Appraisal Data

The best sources of appraisal data are: (1) a knowledgeable individual who has directly and continually observed job performance and who can rate performance without error or bias and (2) items that can be counted, qualified, measured, analyzed, or compared. These factors should be considered no matter which approach is selected for conducting the performance appraisal. This section provides a brief description of the various sources which are currently accepted within organizations. Sources of critical information needed to perform the appraisal function may include: the supervisor, the subordinate, peer review, self-appraisal, and outside appraisals (including the assessment center concept and student evaluations, where applicable).[20]

Supervisor Appraisal

Probably the most important source of judgmental data is the immediate superior. A manager has both a right and a duty to make appraisal and developmental decisions regarding subordinates. In addition, the superior normally assigns the work and is responsible for rewards and sanctions. The liabilities of supervisory appraisal include the familiar objection to "playing God" as well as the lack of interpersonal skills needed to maintain positive relationships with subordinates. Moreover, there is always the possibility of rater errors, including favoritism and bias.

Subordinate Appraisal

Appraisal by subordinates is the opposite of supervisory appraisal and the advantages and disadvantages are reversed. The major advantage is that such appraisals are highly democratic and they encourage participative management. This type of appraisal is often seen as illegitimate because it undermines the superior's rightful authority. Also a superior is already being appraised by subordinates, albeit indirectly. The superior's rating is usually influenced by how well or poorly the subordinates perform their work.

Peer Appraisal

Peer appraisals are most effective when there is a high level of trust among peers and when job performance information is available to peers such as in a faculty.

Research has shown that peer appraisals are strongly correlated with objective measures of job success. However, peer appraisals have a competitive aspect and can be disruptive. Conflicts may arise between making objective appraisals and maintaining collegial relationships. Finally, peers may agree in advance to give each other high ratings.

Self-Appraisal

Self-appraisals may be justified when the individual is in the best position to judge his/her own performance, such as in the case of physical isolation or when the individual possesses a unique skill or ability. Self-appraisals are useful in development because they emphasize personal growth, intrinsic motivation, and goal-setting. They also communicate to the superior how the subordinate perceives his/her performance and provide insights not otherwise available. However, self-appraisals are often poorly correlated with supervisory appraisals and are unreliable as a single source of information for promotions and merit pay.

Appraisal by Outsiders

Appraisal by outsiders is based on the need for someone with specialized expertise but without a vested interest in the appraisal results. Examples are retaining a C.P.A. firm to conduct an audit of a financial statement or a visit by an accreditation team. Another application is known as an assessment center where candidates for managerial positions participate in a variety of situational exercises and are assessed by several trained observers on their performance. Another type of appraisal by outsiders is student evaluation of teaching performance, although the assumptions of specialized expertise and lack of a vested interest do not hold. There is evidence in the literature that suggests that students may sometimes be unable to discriminate between effective and ineffective teaching.[21] Moreover, many faculty members hold somewhat cynical opinions concerning the value of student judgments. Nevertheless, these ratings, when properly evaluated, are a useful source of appraisal data.

In regard to objective data, the variety of measures is so large that it is impossible to categorize them completely. For faculty members the list might include publications, reading lists, community service projects, student clubs, activity reports, test gains, student performance in subsequent courses or other institutions, and the like. For administrators there are accreditation studies, contracts and grants, budgetary increases, management audits, and similar measures. Analogous examples could be cited for support personnel.

Organizational practice and empirical evidence suggest that the appraisal process should normally be conducted by the immediate superior who can integrate both judgmental and quantitative measures. The problems of this approach can be solved by developing a job-related system and by properly training raters. For example, in rating an instructor on the dimension of classroom teaching, the department chair might consider the following:

- Report of a faculty peer review committee

- Analysis of student evaluations

- Recognitions such as testimonials and teaching awards

- Syllabi, manuals, reading lists, and other teaching aids

- Personal observation of classroom performance

- Enrollment and subsequent course performance data

- The instructor's self appraisal

Note that this list includes both judgmental and objective data from a variety of sources.   In rating a different dimension, for example, scholarly productivity, the department chair would develop sources of data which reveal quality, creativity, and significance of the contributions of the professional field.

Cost Considerations

Developing, validating, and administering a performance appraisal system is a major undertaking and requires a substantial investment in time and money.   There are a number of factors an organization should consider in making the decision regarding resources to be invested.   Among these are the nature of the relationship between developmental costs and system effectiveness, allocation of costs among positions, and potential for improving performance.

In general, the more costs the organization is willing to incur, the better the system that can be developed.   It is important to note, however, that as more is invested in development beyond what is necessary to establish validity, incremental costs do not necessarily result in proportionate increases in system effectiveness.   An example would be useful to show this relationship. Assume the objective is to measure the performance of a faculty member. A dimensionalized and weighted rating scale similar to Figure 3.2 could be developed.   Based on the author's experience, the job analysis, criterion development, and instrumentation could be accomplished for under $2,000 and would meet the minimum requirements of the "Guidelines." It might be desired, however, to develop behaviorally anchored rating scales similar to Figure 3.7.   The development of BARS requires a much more sophisticated approach and the cost could be as high as $10,000. While the cost may be five times as high, there is no research which suggests that BARS is five times more accurate. In fact, reviews have not found BARS to produce substantially more accurate results than traditional graphic scales.[22] The same relationship holds true in the administration of a performance appraisal program. The essential elements of such a program include appraisal interviews, and an appeal process. The cost is considerable, and there is always the danger that both subordinates and superiors may spend more time and energy in various aspects of appraisal than in productive work. While certain administrative requirements are necessary, they should be kept in perspective. Beyond the point necessary to ensure that the appraisal program is carried out under standardized and controlled conditions, additional meetings, paperwork and procedures do not justify the cost. In other words, the investment in both development and administration of performance appraisal is subject to diminishing returns.

Another important consideration in the investment decision is the number of incumbents in a particular job category. For example, an institution might have 100 instructional positions and two library technicians. Assume that there are three instructional divisions: e.g., Arts and Humanities, Science and Mathematics, and Nursing. Within each division the instructional positions are fundamentally similar. Thus, the developmental cost of a performance appraisal technique could be spread across 20 to 50 positions in the faculty, but only two in the library. This would support a decision to develop a more sophisticated (and expensive) system for the faculty than for the library and other support departments.

Finally, it is very important to consider the value of post-appraisal benefits in such areas as increased productivity, motivation and satisfaction, staff development, and better administrative decisions. This may be intuitively obvious, but the implications are sometimes overlooked. Thomas F. Gilbert has introduced the concept of potential for improving performance (PIP), which is the ratio of exemplary performance to typical performance.[23] A PIP of 5.0 suggests that typical performance could be improved fivefold, while a PIP of 1.1 tells us that exemplary performance is only 10 percent better than typical performance. Gilbert suggests that in professional athletics PIP's almost invariably run less than 2 and exceptionally competitive and demanding jobs such as that of an airline pilot have PIP's near 1. On the other hand, PIP's in education and government are typically 5 to 30, showing much more potential benefits from performance appraisal.

Concluding Comment

It should be stressed that there is no one best way to go about selecting a performance appraisal technique. Performance appraisal programs serve many purposes, and most of the techniques discussed have valid applications. Organizations may want to eliminate options such as trait rating scales that have serious disadvantages. Several alternatives to the traditional superior-subordinate appraisal review function have been described in this chapter. Organizations may choose to incorporate various sources of information into their overall employee performance appraisal process. They also need to carefully analyze appraisal costs vs. benefits. The methodology finally adopted may be a mixed system with features of several techniques.

Endnotes

1.   Evelyn Eichel and Henry E. Bender, *Performance Appraisal: A survey of Current Techniques*, (New York: American Management Association, 1984), p. 41.

2.   Charles R. Klasson, Duane E. Thompson, and Gary C. Luben, "How Desirable is Your Performance Appraisal System?" *Personnel Administrator* 25 (December 1980), pp. 77-83.

3.   Ronald G. Wells, "Guidelines for Effective and Defensible Performance Appraisal Systems," *Personnel Journal* 61 (October 1982), p. 777.

4.   Eichel and Bender, *op. cit.*, p. 37.

5.   *Ibid.*

6.   William H. Holley and Kenneth M. Jennings, *Personnel Management*, (Chicago: Dryden, 1987), p. 255 and Robert L. Lazar and Walter S. Wikstrom, Appraising Managerial Performance, (New York: Conference Board, 1977), p. 95.

7.   Holley and Jennings, *op. cit.*, p. 256.

8.   Eichel and Bender, *op. cit.*, p. 36.

9.   John C. Flanagan, "The Critical Incident Technique," *Psychological Bulletin* 61 (July 1954), pp. 327-358.

10.   Marion G. Haynes, "Developing an Appraisal Program," *Personnel Journal* 57 (January 1978), pp. 14-19.

11.   Eichel and Bender, *op. cit.*, p. 48.

12.   Gary P. Latham and Kenneth N. Wexley, *Increasing Productivity Through Performance Appraisal*, (Reading, MA: Addison Wesley, 1981), p. 51.

13.   Patricia C. Smith and L. M. Kendall, "Retranslation of Expectations: An Approach to the Construction of Unambiguous Anchors for Rating Scales," *Journal of Applied Psychology* 47 (April 1963), pp. 149-155.

14.   Walter C. Borman, "Effects of Instructions to Avoid Halo Error on Reliability of Performance Evaluation Ratings," *Journal of Applied Psychology* 60 (October 1975), pp. 556-560.

15.   Gary P. Latham and Kenneth N. Wexley, "Behavioral Observation Scales for Performance Appraisal Purposes," *Personnel Psychology* 30 (Summer 1977), pp. 255-268.

16.   Peter F. Drucker, *The Practice of Management*, (New York: Harper and Row, 1954).

17.   For a discussion of the steps in the MBO process see Dale D. McConkey, *How to Manage by Results*, (New York: American Management Associations, 1983), pp. 89-160.

18.   Latham and Wexley, *Increasing Productivity Through Performance Appraisal*, p. 43.

19.   Craig E. Schneier and Richard W. Beatty, "Combining Bars and MBO: Using an Appraisal System to Diagnose Performance Problems," *Personnel Administrator* 24 (September 1979), pp. 51-55.

20.   L. L. Cummings and Donald P. Schwab, "Who Evaluates?" in *The Performance Appraisal Sourcebook*, eds. Lloyd S. Paird, Richard W. Beatty, and Craig E. Schneier (Amherst, MA: Human Resource Development Press, 1982), pp. 81-85 and John B. Bennett and Shirley S. Chater, "Evaluating the Performance of Tenured Faculty Members," *Educational Record* 65 (Spring 1984), pp. 38-41.

21.   Donald W. Miller, "Dangers of Using Student Evaluations for Administrative Purposes," *Collegiate News and Views* 31 (Spring 1978), pp. 2-3 and Irene R. Kiernan, "Student Evaluations Re-Evaluated," *Community and Junior College Journal* 45 (April 1975), pp. 25-27.

22.   See for example, Frank Landy and J. L. Farr, "Performance Rating," *Psychological Bulletin* 87 (January 1980), pp. 88-89.

23.   Thomas F. Gilbert, *Human Competence: Engineering Worthy Performance*, (New York: McGraw-Hill, 1978), pp. 30-43.

4

Development of Performance Appraisal and Accompanying Criteria

Edith A. Miller

The development of an appropriate performance appraisal procedure and its accompanying criteria is a complex set of tasks. While there is a vast body of theory and research related to performance appraisal methodology, there is also an equally extensive and widely differing range of opinion, research, and suggestion in the literature regarding not only performance appraisal generally but also criterion development specifically. While there is no concensus regarding the right or best instrument or the most appropriate criterion, it is clear that whatever form a performance appraisal system takes it must be:

1. Conceptually or philosophically congruent with the job, profession, or constellation of duties and responsibilities it is designed to appraise.

2. Directly related to the actual day-to-day, on-the-job, performance of these duties and responsibilities.

3. Usable and legally defensible.

4. A source of information for improvement (growth) of the individual being assessed as well as improvement or added benefits for the institution or organization in which the individual is employed.

5. Sound from a measurement point-of-view--that is, valid and reliable.

The first four characteristics herein listed are clearly related to a cogent understanding of the job or position to be appraised. Klasson, Thompson, and Luben outlined four important qualities a performance appraisal system must include to be defensible:

1. The performance appraisal system should be formally developed, thoroughly documented, and as objective as possible.

2. The standards of performance for all positions being appraised must be based on the results of a thorough, formal job analysis.

3. Relevant job dimensions and desired job performance should be reflected in each performance standard.

4. The appraisal process should involve the measurement of performance with the weighting of each dimension or criterion fixed prior to the utilization of the appraisal system.[1]

Throughout these qualities is found the notion that the performance appraisal procedure is inextricably linked to the nature of the job or performance being appraised. The preferred method for assuring that the performance appraisal is not only conceptually and philosophically congruent but also directly related to the actual performance being appraised is some form of job or task analysis. The first section of this chapter will address job analysis as it serves as the basis for the development of the overall performance appraisal system and most specifically for the development of the evaluative criteria with which the system operates. Issues surrounding the choice, adaptation, and/or development of a performance appraisal system will be explored in the second section of the chapter. Specific measurement issues regarding performance appraisal with specific attention to reliability and validity as well as sources of error will conclude this chapter.

Job Analysis

The issue of job analysis is as central to the development of tests, performance appraisals, and evaluation procedures as it is to the development of management strategies. Ghorpode defined job analysis as ". . . a managerial activity directed at gathering, analyzing, and synthesizing information about jobs."[2] Lopez, Kesselman, and Lopez indicated that from the time it began to assume importance in the test construction process, job analysis had also begun to play an important role in personnel selection.[3]

Both the process and outcome of job analysis are essential to the development of a performance appraisal system. Not only does the job analysis information serve as the base for the development of the "items" or "behaviors" or "traits" to be appraised but also a well designed and executed job analysis will contribute to criterion development and content validation. Moreover, it was shown in Chapter 2 that job analysis has compelling legal implications.

The job analysis procedure is in itself a complex and demanding aspect of the development of a performance appraisal system. Prien strongly stated that job analysis is not an easy job that just "anybody" can do.[4] Rather it is a step that requires much thorough planning and careful execution. He further indicated that while the research on job analysis techniques has indeed grown beyond its infancy, there is still not a strong body of research to answer the question of what is the best job analysis procedure to use in specific situations.[5] In *Principles for the Validation and Use of Personnel Selection Procedures*, the following statement is made that, "There is currently no authoritative set of principles for job analysis comparable to the Standards or Principles in the area of selection procedures."[6] The document continued by noting some specific things that a job analysis must do: (1) specify the descriptors or units of analysis by which the job will be defined, (2) develop task or activity statements for job-oriented analyses, and (3) develop behavioral statements or descriptors for worker-oriented analyses.

The categorization of job analyses into job-oriented and worker-oriented is very useful.   There are literally dozens of published job analysis procedures.   Bemis, Belensky, and Soder reviewed ten such systems as bases for developing a system which draws on both job-oriented techniques and worker-oriented techniques--Versatile Job Analysis System (VERJAS).[7] The systems discussed by the authors range from the widely-used and generally well respected Department of Labor (DOL) procedure to the Guidelines Oriented Job Analysis (GOJA) which was developed specifically in response to legal and regulatory requirements.

To discuss a wide variety of these job analysis procedures goes well beyond the scope of this document. However, it is important to have an understanding of the ways in which the job-oriented and worker-oriented models differ. Ghorpode stated that the job-oriented models tend to draw on the system framework for their definition.[8] The analysis of a specific job is seen as the analysis of a sub-unit of the organization. Sidney Fine's Functional Job Analysis (FJA) is a good example of this particular model. Worker-oriented systems rest on preconceptions about the nature of the inter-relations between the aspects of the job and the individual in that position. The Position Analysis Questionnaire (PAQ) is a good example of the worker-oriented model. To explore the differences between these two approaches to job analyses, the FJA and the PAQ will be examined in more detail. Because of the importance of legal considerations, a brief discussion of GOJA will also be presented.

Sidney Fine's Functional Job Analysis, developed during and after World War II, rests on a "systematically articulated theory of jobs and people":[9]

1. A fundamental distinction must be made between what gets done and what workers do to get things done.

2. What workers do, insofar as job content is concerned, they do in relation to three primitives: things, data, and people.

3. In relation to each primitive, workers function in unique ways. Thus, in relation to things, workers draw on physical resources; in relation to data, on mental resources; and in relation to people, on interpersonal resources.

4. All jobs require the worker to relate to each of these primitives in some degree.

5. Although the behavior of workers or the tasks performed by them can apparently be described in an infinite number of ways, there are only a small number of definitive functions involved. thus, in interacting with machines, workers function to feed, tend, operate, or set up; and in the case of vehicles or related machines, to drive-control them. Although each of these functions occurs over a range of difficulty and content, essentially each draws on a relatively narrow and specific range of similar kinds and degrees of worker characteristics and qualifications for effective performance.

6. The functions appropriate to each primitive are hierarchical and ordinal, proceeding from the simple to the complex. Thus, to indicate a particular function, compiling (data), for example, as reflecting the requirements of a job is to say that it includes the requirements of lower functions such as comparing and excludes the requirement of higher functions such as analyzing.

7. The three hierarchies provide two measures for a job: Level is a measure of relative complexity in relation to things, to data, and to people. Orientation is a measure of relative (proportional) involvement with things, data, and people.

8. The hierarchies of functions reflect a progression from much prescription and little discretion in worker instruction at the least complex level to much discretion and little prescription at the most complex level.

9. Human performance is conceived as involving three types of skills: adaptive, functional, and specific content. Adaptive skills are those competencies that enable an individual to manage the demands for conformity and/or change in relation to the physical, interpersonal, and organizational arrangements and conditions in which the job exists. Functional skills are those competencies that enable an individual to relate to things, data, and people (orientation) in some combination according to personal preferences and to come degree of complexity appropriate to abilities (level). Specific content skills are those competencies that enable an individual to perform a specific job according to standards required to satisfy the market.[10]

The Position Analysis Questionnaire (PAQ) was specifically designed to be a worker-oriented model. Developed by Ernest J. McCormick and his associates at Purdue University, the PAQ is based on the following underlying assumption.

If there is some such underlying behavioral structure, such structure presumably would have to be characterized in terms of the manner in which more specific "units" of job-related variables tend to be organized across jobs. Thus, the "building blocks" or common denominators or any dimensional structure must consist of relatively unitary, discrete job variables of some class that can be identified and quantified as they relate to individual jobs.[11]

An inventory of "job elements" within major divisions and subdivisions is then proposed in the PAQ. Within these divisions the inventory of job elements serve as a basis for determining the behavioral dimensions of jobs. These dimensions include: (1 information input, (2) mental processes, (3) work output, (4) relationships with other persons, (5) job context, and (6) other job characteristics. In regard to job context or the physical or social contexts in which the work occurs, examples of job elements would be high temperature and interpersonal conflict situations.

A method which specifically addresses the requirements of the "Uniform Guidelines" is known as GOJA, an acronym for Guidelines Oriented Job Analysis.[12] This method, developed in 1974 by Richard E. Biddle, has been periodically refined and updated and has been successfully used with numerous public and private employees.

When implemented in its entirety, GOJA is a multistep process which results in a selection plan. For purposes of performance appraisal the earlier steps of the process deal with the identification and characteristics of job duties as shown below:

1. Collection preliminary job data.

2. Identify major job duties.

3. Rate each duty by frequency and importance.

4. Cluster related duties into job domains.

These steps represent about one-half of the GOJA process; however, they provide the foundation on which a performance appraisal system can be built. GOJA is one of the few methods available that systematically takes a user from the content of a job to the content of a performance appraisal instrument. GOJA's thoroughness in application and documentation makes it an important and useful method.[13]

These rather disparate examples of job analysis procedures should make the point that one must very carefully design the specific job analysis to meet the purposes to which the resulting data will be applied. The APA Principles suggested that job analysis procedures ". . . be chosen or developed as it is appropriate to obtain job information for the purposes or application of that job analysis information."[14] Pearlman suggested an examination of the research and conceptual issues in the area before choosing an approach.[15]

Ghorpode indicated that from the more job-oriented approaches one would get information about job outputs, guidelines, controls, tasks, and other job factors.[16] With the more worker-oriented systems, information about aptitudes, abilities, and other human characteristics would emerge. The degree to which the appraisal system is designed to focus on these two dimensions of job analysis will direct the nature of the procedure. Just as the job analysis procedure can be oriented toward the job or the worker, it can also be oriented toward qualitative or quantitative data. The range of data gathered in job analyses extends from truly narrative, anecdotal records to highly quantitative data that can be totally analyzed with a computer. Again, the design of the job analysis will determine the kind of data gathered.

Development Issues

A variety of development issues arises when one considers either adopting, adapting, or developing a performance appraisal procedure. The first and most important of these issues is the determination of the purpose of the appraisal procedure--the use of the resulting data. If the purpose of procedure is to make large-scale summative, institutional judgments, one's focus would be quite different than if the focus were to identify strengths and weaknesses with a view toward employee growth and development. Each of these widely differing purposes and many purposes between these two examples will serve to establish the frame-of-reference for the choice, adaptation, or development of a performance appraisal procedure.

As indicated in regard to job analyses procedures, there is also no clearly superior approach to conducting performance appraisals. There is a vast amount of research and theory around the issue, and depending on one's purpose, some of the research can be helpful in choosing an approach. As an illustration for this discussion of development issues, the use of a rating scale approach to performance appraisal will be used. Rating scales have proved to be generally useful in performance appraisal, and depending on the nature and use of the scale have also proved to be reliable. A study by Dawes indicated that while most rating scales are non-representational, with appropriate directions a rating scale could be used reliably to measure a representation variable, height.[17] Furthermore, rating scales have both ordinal and interval properties.[18]

The retranslation method has provided a useful approach to establishing rating scales with behavioral anchors.[19] The accuracy of a rating scale format will, of course, vary with the nature of the job or performance being appraised.[20] However, a variety of rating scale formats--Behavioral Expectation Scale (BES), Behaviorally Anchored Rating Scale (BARS), and Behavioral Observation Scale (BOS)--is being used extensively and very appropriately in performance appraisal activity.

In 1963, Maurice Lorr, C. James Klett, and Douglas McNair made five specific suggestions regarding the development of rating scales:

1. Only one variable should be rated at a time.

2. Several items covering an aspect of behavior or a trait should be included in a rating scale.

3. Scales should allow the rater to describe the strength of a trait or behavior. Bipolar opposites are difficult to depend on for clear information.

4. Items should use clear, non-jargon language as much as possible.

5. The span of the scale should reflect the range expected in the population to be appraised.[21]

In discussing the construction of rating instruments for faculty evaluation, Berk maintained that the characteristics of the instrument would evolve from four basic phases of the construction process:

1. Specification of the domain.

2. Scaling of the instrument.

3. Item generation.

4. Statistical analysis of the instrument.[22]

Domain specification is, of course, the identification of the "ballpark" of the appraisal development process. What skills, behaviors, performances, traits, abilities, qualities, aspects, etc. will the appraisal address? The development of the criteria (criterion) against which these aspects will be appraised is also of critical importance. Flanagan, in describing the critical incident technique of performance appraisal, suggested that the criteria for performance appraisal must come not only from qualified experts but also from descriptions of skilled professionals. The steps proposed by Flanagan included the following:

1. Observation of the activity's purpose of aim.

2. Specification of the observation methodology.

3. Data collection.

4. Analysis of observation data.

5. Interpretation of resulting data to establish performance criteria.[23]

In the specification of the domain to be assessed, Berk suggested a procedure called facet analysis: "The task of the domain deemed important and worthy of measurement."[24] The purpose of an appraisal system and the anticipated use of the resulting information will, of course, determine how general or specific this facet analysis must be. The developmental step which follows the identification of the facets of the domain is to translate them into a set of elements which identify the salient features of the performance to be appraised. Berk suggested a set of guidelines for the development of rating instruments.[25] Many of these points are directly relevant to the development of a rating scale within a performance appraisal system.

1. Specify the purposes of the evaluation (appraisal) and the decisions to be made with the results.

2. Define the domain of characteristics to be measured using facet analysis or a similar procedure.

3. Develop a summated rating scale continuum consistent with the types of characteristics to be rated.

    a. Intensity of scale is in Likert form of agreement/disagreement.
    b. Numerical format should be used rather than graphic when possible because of scoring or summing ease.
    c. Anchors of scale should be clearly defined.
    d. Five-point scale is adequate from the point of reliability.
    e. Neutral option on the scale can be used or not according to personal preference.
    f. Non-applicable option should be used only for non-applicable items.

4. Generate a pool of items to measure the characteristics.

    a. Two or three items per facet.
    b. Available rating instruments and banks serving as resource.
    c. Evaluating items for quality and congruence with domain specifications.

5. Field-test the instrument and appraise the psychometric qualities of validity, reliability, item stability, etc.

Using this general format suggested by Berk is a straightforward approach to rating scale development.[26] Berk's general steps, however, apply to the development of other appraisal measures as well. Once the rating scale, or checklist or inventory of tasks, has been developed, Berk suggested the following criteria for evaluating items:

Content/Format:

1. Clear, direct, specific language.
2. One complete thought or concept.
3. Concise (no more than 20 words).
4. Simple sentence.
5. No universal words, e.g., all, always, none, never.
6. No words like only, just, and merely.
7. No jargon.

Congruence with Specifications:

8. Applicable to all being evaluated.
9. A desirable characteristic.
10. Congruent with facet element.

11.   Consistent with anchors on rating scale.

12.   Factual or can be interpreted as factual.

13.   Open to only one interpretation.

14.   Likely to be responded to by all raters.[27]

Beyond these simple criteria against which to compare the items on the instrument itself, the items should also be compared against the scale to be used. Berk suggested a summated (Likert) scale.[28] Other scales which might be considered include: paired comparisons, equal appearing intervals, successive intervals, scalogram analysis, semantic differential, Q-sort techniques, and multidimensional scaling. Some of these procedures have serious drawbacks regarding the reliability and validity of the resulting data--paired comparisons, for example. Again, the scale should be chosen in light of the intended use of the resulting data. The summated scale (Likert-type) does lend itself to statistical analyses that go beyond simple descriptive statistics.

Once the domain has been specified drawing on-the-job analysis information, an instrument type and scale have been chosen, and items have been developed, the next consideration is the statistical analyses of the resulting data. There are two major arenas of statistical analyses to be considered: (1) analyses of the data in the instrument development process and (2) the analysis of the resulting data for decision or staff development use.

Three major types of analyses should be conducted at the instrument development stage: (1) intercorrelations of items, (2) study of variability, and (3) factor analysis of the items and subscales to test for empirical verification of conceptual item development.

The analysis of the resulting data depends on the kinds of decisions to be made with the data. There is much controversy about whether performance appraisal instruments should be one dimensional or should represent several dimensions. Again, the literature provides no clear-cut answer. However, Smith clearly indicated that ". . . when several dimensions are involved several sets of criteria as composites will be required."[29] Given the highly specific nature of performance appraisals, one answer to the question of one overall measure or a series of discrete measures is absolutely impossible. The analyses of these data would, of course, help in determining the relatedness or independence of the various dimensions of the instrument.

Whether one adds all of the items into one scale or related items into subscales, Fralicx and Raju found that the weighting of items need not be as difficult as once thought.[30] In their study of 112 bankers, they found that Management Weights (MGR), Equal Weights (EQL), Unit Weights (UNIT), and Factor Weights (FACT) produce highly comparable ratings. Equal weights derived by utilizing standard deviation reciprocals and management weights achieved by having managers weight each item are considerably more time consuming than allowing each item to contribute equally to the sum. Likewise, factor analysis is more time-consuming and requires much more sophistication. A fifth weighting procedure--canonical correlation--was also used in the study, but those weighted results correlated roughly at the zero level with the other weights.   Because of the nature of canonical correlation, that particular result was expected by the researchers.

Decisions made on the weighted, summed, or otherwise statistically or conceptually treated data must be made by those who designed the performance appraisal system.   Standard setting and cut-scores, numbers of items at particular levels, and levels of performance required must be determined in terms of local needs.   One caution that all using performance appraisal instruments must heed, however, is that many of the traits, behaviors, attributes, aptitudes, etc. that are being appraised are not parallel either in importance or in ease of measurement or observation.   These considerations must be attended to in any performance appraisal approach.

Measurement Considerations

The primary measurement considerations which come to mind when focusing on performance appraisal are those of validity and reliability.   Does the performance appraisal system indeed tap those dimensions of the performance that are criterial to the effective job performance?   Bailey suggested that there are three approaches to determining whether or not the criterion of effective job performance is indeed being measured: (1) job analytic procedures, [31,32,33] (2) performance/factor analytic approaches,[31,34] and (3) appraiser-generated approaches.[31,35]   If, in the development or adaptation of the performance appraisal procedure at least two of those dimensions could be utilized, the initial notion of content validity would be addressed.   Additional content validation can be achieved by ratings of experts, but the primary sources of content validation are the conceptual validation of the job analysis and the empirical validation of the factor analytic approaches.

While content validity lacks the quantitative rigor of other methods, it would be erroneous to conclude that this method of validation is inferior, particularly with performance appraisal.   What is central to the concept is that the performance measures appropriately sample the domain of job content.   When these measures are developed through comprehensive job analysis, the "inferential leap" between the content of the performance measure and the content of the job is minimized.[36]   The "Uniform Guidelines" accord equal status to content validation alone when behaviors and outcomes are directly observable.[37]   Finally, in that focus is on the measure itself, rather than on external variables, content validity is often the only practical choice.

Criterion-related validity is, of course, always considered appropriate.   There are some problems with predictive validity in regard to the item and resources necessary to conduct the longitudinal study necessary for predictive studies.   If the concurrent study is conducted with on-the-job employees as the criterion respondents to the instrument there are serious problems as the criterion respondents to the instrument, there are serious problems with the employees not being directly similar to prospective employees, with their having learned on-the-job, and with their experiencing lower levels o test anxiety. While this is valuable information, such concurrent studies must be viewed with caution.

Cautions are in order regarding face validity.[38,39] While an instrument appearing to measure what it is designed to measure is indeed a strong public relations factor, one must be most careful about the emphasis given to claims of face validity and to the qualifications of those making the face validity judgments. Nonetheless, an instrument which appears to be relevant certainly meets with more acceptance than does one that seems foreign or unrelated to one's job performance.

The final validity issue that might be addressed is that of convergent/discriminant validity.[40] With multiple measures of many of the traits, attributes, and behaviors contained in a performance appraisal process, such a validity study is most appropriate.

The reliability issue regarding performance appraisals must be addressed from two perspectives: (1) reliability of the instrument and (2) inter-rater reliability. Osgood, Succi, and Tannenbaum used factor analytic studies to test for internal consistency.[41] Currently, the coefficient alpha is in wide use to test for internal consistency.[42]

The issue of inter-rater reliability is a serious consideration, and the primary variable affecting it is training in the use of the procedure. That issue is addressed in Chapter 6, which focuses on minimizing rater errors.

Endnotes

1. Charles R. Klasson, Duane E. Thompson, and Gary L. Luben, "How Defensible is Your Performance Appraisal System?" *Personnel Administrator* 25 (December 1980), pp. 77-83.

2. Jai Gharpode, *Job Analysis: A Handbook for the Human Resource Director* (Englewood Cliffs, NJ: Prentice-Hall, 1988), p. 1.

3. Felix M. Lopez, Gerald A. Kesselman, and Felix E. Lopez," An Empirical Test of a Trait-Oriented Job Analysis Technique," *Personnel Psychology* 34 (Autumn 1981), pp. 479-502.

4. Erich P. Prien, "The Function of Job Analysis in Content Validation," *Personnel Psychology* 30 (Summer 1977), pp. 167-174.

5. *Ibid.*

6. American Psychological Association, Division of Industrial-Organizational Psychology, *Principles for the Validation and Use of Personnel Selection Procedures* 2nd ed. (Berkeley, CA: Author, 1980), p. 4.

7. Stephen E. Bemis, Ann H. Belensky, and Dee A. Soder, *Job Analysis--An Effective Management Tool* (Washington, DC: The Bureau of National Affairs, 1983).

8. Gharpode, *op. cit.*, pp. 232-233.

9. *Ibid.*

10.   Sidney A. Fine and W. W. Wiley, *An Introduction to Functional Job Analysis: A Scaling of Selected Tasks from the Social Welfare Field* (Kalamazoo, MI: W. E. Upjohn Institute for Employment Research, 1971), pp. 78-80.

11.   Ernest J. McCormick, Paul R. Jeanneret, and Robert C. Mecham, "A Study of Job Characteristics and Job Dimensions as Based on the Position Analysis Questionnaire (PAQ)," *Journal of Applied Psychology* 56 (August 1972), pp. 347-367.

12.   Richard E. Biddle, *Guidelines Oriented Job Analysis* (Sacramento: Biddle and Associates, 1982).

13.   Robert D. Gatewood and Hubert L. Field, *Human Resource Selection* (Chicago: Dryden, 1987), p. 231.

14.   American Psychological Association, *op. cit.*, p. 5.

15.   Kenneth Pearlman, "Job Families: A Review and Discussion of Their Implications for Personnel Selection," *Psychological Bulletin* 87 (January 1980), pp. 1-28.

16.   Gharpode, *op. cit.*

17.   Robyn M. Dawes, "Suppose We Measured Height With Rating Scales Instead of Rulers," *Applied Psychological Measurement* 1 (Spring 1977), pp. 267-273.

18.   Graham K. Kenny, "The Metric Properties of Rating Scales Employed in Evaluation Research," *Evaluation Review* 10 (June 1986), pp. 397-408.

19.   Michael J. Kavanagh and John F. Duffy, "An Extension and Field Test of the Retranslation Method for Developing Rating Scales," *Personnel Psychology* 31 (Autumn 1978), pp. 461-470.

20.   Walter C. Borman, "Format and Training Effects of Rater Accuracy and Rater Errors," *Journal of Applied Psychology* 64 (August 1979), pp. 410-421.

21.   Maurice Lorr, C. James Klett, and Douglas M. McNair, *Syndromes of Psychosis* (New York: Pergamon Press, 1963).

22.   Ronald A. Berk, "The Construction of Rating Instruments for Faculty Evaluation: A Review of Methodological Issues," *Journal of Higher Education* 50 (September-October 1979), pp. 650-669.

23.   John C. Flanagan, "The Critical Incident Technique," *Psychological Bulletin* 51 (July 1954), pp. 327-358.

24.   Berk, *op. cit.*, p. 652.

25.   *Ibid.*, p. 664.

26.   Ronald A. Berk, "Empirical Evaluation of Formulae for Correction of Item-Total Point-Biserial Correlations," *Educational and Psychological Measurement* 38 (Fall 1978), pp. 647-652.

27.   *Ibid.*

28.   *Ibid.*

29. Cited from Catherine T. Bailey, *The Measurement of Job Performance* (Aldershot, England: Gower, 1983), p. 748.

30. Rodney D. Fralicx and Nambury S. Raju, "A Comparison of Five Methods for Combining Multiple Criteria into a Single Composite," *Educational and Psychological Measurement* 42 (Autumn 1982), pp. 823-827.

31. Catherine T. Bailey, *The Measurement of Job Performance* (Aldershot, England: Gower, 1983).

32. Flanagan, *op. cit.*, pp. 327-358.

33. Bryant F. Nagle, "Criterion Development," *Personnel Psychology* 6 (Autumn 1953), pp. 271-289.

34. Robert M. Guoin, "Criterion Measurement and Personnel Judgement," *Personnel Psychology* 14 (Spring 1961), pp. 141-149.

35. Patricia Smith and Lorne M. Kendall, "Retranslation of Expectations: An Approach to the Construction of Unambiguous Anchors for Rating Scales," *Journal of Applied Psychology* 47 (February 1963), pp. 149-155.

36. Gatewood and Field, *op. cit.*, p. 135.

37. "Uniform Guidelines on Employee Selection Procedures," *Federal Register* 43 (August 25, 1978), pp. 38302-38303.

38. Baruch Nevo, "Face Validity Revisited," *Journal of Educational Measurement* 22 (Winter 1985), pp. 287-293.

39. Charles Secolsky, "On the Direct Measurement of Face Falidity: A Comment on Nevo," *Journal of Educational Measurement* 24 (Spring 1987), pp. 82-83.

40. Donald T. Campbell and Donald W. Fiske, "Convergent and Discriminant Validation by the Multitrait-Multimethod Matrix," *Psychological Bulletin* 56 (January 1959), pp. 81-105.

41. Charles E. Osgood, George J. Succi, and Percy H. Tannenbaum, *The Measurement of Meaning* (Urbana, IL: University of Illinois Press, 1957).

42. Lee J. Cronbach, *Essentials of Psychological Testing* 4th ed., (New York: Harper and Row, 1984).

5

Communication Factors in Appraisal

Mark E. Meadows

Supervisors in many organizations see little practical value in conducting performance appraisals.[1]   This attitude may be exacerbated in postsecondary education settings where administrators are first and foremost scholars within increasingly narrow disciplines and not always skilled or expert in managerial functions.   Performance appraisal systems have yielded disappointing results within the community college environment; even so, effecting such a system is significant to the success of community colleges.[2]

Saliance of Communication to Performance Appraisal

There is mounting evidence that success or failure of performance appraisal rests on the effectiveness of the terminal appraisal event; that is, the appraisal interview.[3] Laird and Clampitt cited research which suggested that performance review interviews make employees more defensive and self-conscious about their job behavior.[4] Goodall, Wilson, and Waagen claimed that fear of what performance appraisals might yield keeps the appraisal process from achieving its full potential.[5] Appraisers experience high levels of anxiety when giving negative feedback[6] and futility because they either do not believe they can do what is required of them in performance appraisals or that the environment will not be responsible to their efforts.[7] For appraisees, "The performance appraisal interview is a situation that determines . . . survival or death."[8] Clearly, performance appraisal interviews are complex, potentially charged situations which call for appraiser communication skills of the highest order.

Maier recommended that performance appraisal issues be approached as communication problems. He contended, "The success or failure of an employee development program largely depends on the skill with which employees are interviewed by their supervisors."[9] At its simplest level, the performance appraisal interview is a communication event in which two persons attempt to exchange meanings through spoken words.   Regrettably, simplicity in communication is quickly lost in complexity. Norman Cousins, a former *Saturday Review* editor, concluded a highly publicized conflict with exasperation: "The most difficult and precarious enterprise in the world is communication. It is the ultimate act."[10]

It has long been claimed that communication is the number one problem in management.[11] It should follow that managers and supervisors must assume responsibility to see that effective communication takes place in appraisal interviews. As the more expert or more accountable person, the supervisor needs to establish conditions that are conducive to effective communication and model good communication skills in appraisal interviews. Communication is the only technique managers have for exchanging meaning with subordinates. How else can the supervisor explore job performance with an employee; provide an employee with feedback on how closely work quality approximates expectations; dispense important, though intangible, rewards for jobs well done; or establish goals? The performance appraisal interview is considered the primary context for supervisors and employers to work together to achieve superior performance.[12]

Napier and Latham are among researchers in performance appraisal who have detected a shift in research from foci emphasizing psychometric qualities of rating and evaluation instruments to a focus on the appraiser.[13] Although they emphasize complex social learning theory in explaining appraiser interview behaviors, Napier and Latham are only two among numerous writers and researchers in performance appraisal who place emphasis on the key role of communication variables in performance appraisal. Communication between appraiser and appraisee is affected by fears of what performance appraisals might yield. Goodall, Wilson, and Waagen focus on the hierarchical nature of such communication; that is, communication between a superior and a subordinate.[14] Wexley described two primary objectives of the appraisal interview; both accomplished through communication variables. He gave special attention to the direction of communication flow in organizations. Because the flow is usually downward, distortion, inaccuracy, and suspicion result. Wexley's view of appraiser role is that of a helper whose primary role is communication.[15] Stano focused on appraiser communication skills and the importance of appraisee participation in discussion as factors affecting the quality of performance appraisals.[16] Laird and Clampitt identified dissemination of results through the interview as one of four major problems in conducting performance appraisals.[17]

Review of research related to performance appraisal, and especially that which deals with problems encountered, makes abundantly clear the fact that appraiser-appraisee interaction variables--communication if you will--account in large part for the success or failure of performance appraisal systems. Given that fact, and accepting as an assumption that the supervisor/appraiser has the primary responsibility to see that good communication takes place, the remainder of this chapter is devoted to two topics: (1) a brief description of key communication concepts and (2) communication problems inherent in performance appraisal, together with suggestions for mitigating communication problems.

Communication Concepts

Communication may be defined as the process of exchanging meaning between persons. Person A, the sender or encoder, conveys a message to Person B, the receiver or decoder, who interprets the message and responds (encodes) in some way to let Person A know that the message has been received. When Person B decodes and interprets A's message the simplest form of interpersonal communication has taken place. For the purpose of reinforcing the fact that the leader must take responsibility to insure that effective communication occurs in the performance appraisal process, it will be helpful if readers identify themselves as persons encoding, or sending, verbal messages in the content that follows, that is, as Person A. Figure 5.1 depicts the basic communication transaction which occurs in any form of communication, including performance appraisal.

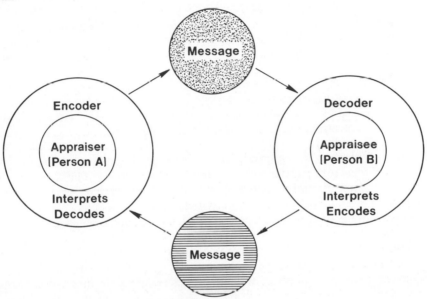

Fig. 5.1. Basic Communication Transaction

Frequently, appraisers sending messages find that their purposes are not achieved; the receiver (appraisee) does not respond as expected or possibly does not respond at all. When communication is viewed simply as "sending" a message, we may safely assume that communication will not take place. As with the Tango, communication is a two-way process. It takes two people to hold an effective performance discussion.[18] Further, the two persons must be in contact, have each other's attention, and attach similar meanings to messages. In summary, there must be a sender who transmits a message to a receiver who understands the meaning of the message in the same sense as the sender. The sender ascertains that communication has taken place by securing feedback from the receiver. Only then can the sender know whether a message has been accurately communicated or whether the message needs to be revised and encoded again. Wexley described as one of two primary objectives of appraisal interviews feedback to appraisees.[19]

Feedback is especially important when the purpose of communication is instrumental; that is, to obtain a behavioral response from the receiver of the message. When such messages are sent, feedback is best obtained by asking, "Now, tell me what you are going to do." The supervisor needs to know what is understood by the supervisee. When a subordinate is asked, "Do you understand?" there is considerable pressure to answer, "Yes." Otherwise, one's superior might think one is not intelligent.

We communicate best with those who have experiences similar to our own; however, few persons enjoy the luxury of communicating with a narrow range of persons altogether similar to themselves. In Figure 5.1, the messages of A and B are shaded differently to communicate the fact that their experiential backgrounds will "shade" their messages. Employees of higher educational institutions now represent a broader range of cultural, ethnic, and socioeconomic background than in the past.[20] Communicator differences in experiential background can cause senders and receivers to attach quite different meanings to the same words and objects to the extent that messages sent are not identical to messages received. Sensitivity and efforts to increase knowledge of diverse groups are called for. Appraisers who wish to improve communication must learn to hear messages from the "frame of reference" of others.

The needs of those communicating can cause breakdown in communication. The sender may feel a need to put the receiver "in his or her place." The receiver may feel threatened when communicating with the sender. Both sender and receiver can enhance the likelihood of effective communication by being as aware as possible of both his/her own needs and those of the person with whom they communicate; however, this is especially a responsibility of the leader/appraiser. Such awareness can reduce defensive behavior and rid the interaction of communication distortions that defensiveness elicits and sustains. Figure 5.2 represents two basic needs of every person, the need to protect oneself and the need to enhance oneself. When these needs are threatened or thwarted communication will break down.

It is important to communication effectiveness that senders communicate clearly their expectations. In most performance appraisal interviews appraisers send messages that attempt to elicit a behavioral response, that is, an instrumental response. Unless senders make expectations explicit, the desired response will not be forthcoming. There is appreciable evidence in support of the so-called Pygmalion effect, that persons generally respond to expectations. However, if expectations are not clear and responses are not those sought, inappropriate assumptions about the competency of a subordinate may be made when, in fact, that assumption is not justified.

Beliefs of both sender and receiver create difficulties in communication. Napier and Latham draw from social learning theory to identify two cognitive variables which are sources of futility experienced by appraisers, self-efficacy and outcome expectations.[21] Appraisers who believe they cannot do what is required of them (low self-efficacy) experience feelings of futility because they do not believe the environment will be responsive to their efforts; they have poor outcome expectations. In either case belief systems of communicators can interfere with communication.

Attitudes are as potent as beliefs in creating communication difficulties. Supervisors communicate a certain attitude when they confer with supervisees only on their own turf rather than in the supervisee's workplace or a neutral setting. Communication across the physical barrier of a supervisor's desk does not improve understanding.[22] Figure 5.3 is an attempt to depict some of the multiple human factors that are constantly affecting the flow of messages between two persons. Again, the appraiser must assume primary responsibility for recognizing the impact of these factors and in reducing any negative impact they have in communicating with appraisers.

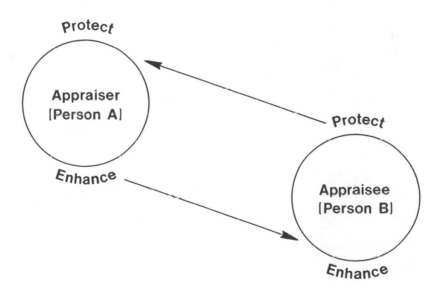

Fig. 5.2. Two Basic Needs Affecting Communication

Finally, poor listeners make poor communicators. All too often, simple failure to listen is the cause of communication breakdown. Two poor listening habits predominate as communication barriers. One of these is the tendency to attach evaluative judgments to what others say. Rather than listening, the receiver is making judgments, filtering the message, and thereby failing to receive all the meaning intended by the sender. One method for breaking this habit is for the appraiser/supervisor to adopt the non-evaluative feedback rule. Before the appraiser responds to an appraisee statement, the message must be repeated by the appraiser until the appraisee recognizes that both the content and feelings expressed are understood.[23] The tendency to listen evaluatively contributes to another poor listening habit. Instead of attending fully to what the sender is saying, the receiver may be forming responses. When receivers are preoccupied with how they will respond to points being made by senders, the points are usually missed. Stano advocated that managers be taught to listen carefully and accurately, to give reflective feedback, and to ask appropriate, open-ended, non-directive questions. Stano felt that careful listening was especially important in encouraging subordinates to talk.[24]

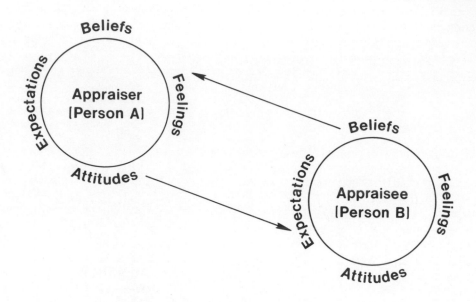

Fig. 5.3. Factors Affecting the Flow of Messages Between Persons

Performance Appraisal Situations With Inherent Communication Problems

The performance appraisal interview is rife with situations which have potential for communication breakdown. These include the hierarchical nature of such events, [25] inherently evaluative aspects of performance appraisal, multiple purposes of some appraisal interviews,[26] influence of the environmental climate, including non-verbal aspects of performance appraisal interviews.[27] Each of these special situations is discussed below in terms of the unique communication problem(s) posed, together with suggestions for mitigating communication breakdown.

Burke identified the "mystery" that surrounds hierarchical communication, ". . . the conditions for 'mystery' are set by any pronounced social distinction . . . the social distinction between clerk and office/manager makes them subtly mysterious to each other, not merely two different people, but representing two classes or 'kinds' of people."[28] The existence of mystery between classes of beings points out an essential quality of the performance appraisal interview: a superior will be communicating with an inferior in the organization. Goodall, Wilson, and Waagen pointed out that when mystery intercedes in communication between different classes of beings, the common response is to retreat to ritual forms of address; that is, communicative behaviors that are guided by commonly understood cultural and social stereotypes, traditional etiquette, gender-specific, or race-specific rules.[29] Both interviewer and interviewee are encouraged to rely on and to respond to prepackaged scripts for the situation that derive rules from commonly understood cultural values and standards.[30] "In short, the mystery present in the situation is reinforced by ritual forms of communication."[31] In the face of pressures to retreat to fixed, conventional forms of communication between appraiser/appraisee, the appraiser must assume responsibility to assure that the barrier is broken and that honest, open communication occurs.

Although some experts in performance appraisal advocate that managers treat employees as equals,[32] it does not follow that the employee will adopt this attitude or that such attempts of managers will be credible, especially if the manager's behavior is not consistent with past behavior.[33] Review of the literature suggests that the primary way to reduce the "mystery" in supervisor/subordinate communication is to facilitate participation of the subordinate; the manager needs skills that encourages subordinates to talk.[34] Participation is encouraged through active listening,[35] manager behaviors that are spontaneous, friendly, sensitive, that show interest in subordinates, and that are nonjudgmental.[36] The best place for the appraisal interview is a neutral setting and not in the manager's office, thus reducing the distance over which communication occurs. Finally, Goodall et al. discussed the central purpose of performance appraisal interviews from the frame of reference of both the supervisor and the subordinate.[37] They stressed the need for clarity of purpose of the appraisal for each party. When there is a common understanding of what the parameters of the performance interview are, the appraisee is more likely to experience the safety required for self-disclosure and risk-taking, thereby making the interview a more authentic, spontaneous experience. Bellman stated, "A performance discussion without objectives is not a performance discussion."[38] In summary, the negative effects of status differences on communication within the performance interview are mitigated when the appraiser (1) assumes responsibility to see that effective communication occurs, (2) listens carefully, (3) clarifies interview purposes and goals, and (4) involves the appraisee in all phases of performance appraisal, including the design of the program.[39] When possible, the employer should be allowed to rate his own performance.[40]

The fact that performance appraisals exist in part to provide evaluative feedback to appraisees constitutes another critical communication variable in performance appraisal. Bennett and Chater underscored this aspect of appraisal in postsecondary settings. They cited several current concerns in higher education that have led faculty and administrators alike to tighten their judgments. Bennett and Chater especially made a case for evaluating the performance of tenured faculty in order to foster and maintain excellent performance.[41] It is noteworthy that virtually no literature on performance appraisal posits a view that does not include the evaluative nature of performance appraisal.

Given that evaluation either takes place or that existing evaluation data are presented in appraisal interviews, what can be done to reduce its negative impact? Three basic communication techniques that have potential to reduce the negative effects of employee evaluation in the performance interview are offered: feedback clarification, non-evaluative listening, and achieving an appropriate balance of praise and criticism. It should be noted again that the interviewer/supervisor must assume responsibility to use such techniques, although employees can also be taught these skills.

Non-evaluative listening involves receiving communication from an appraisee without placing any value judgment on the message or the sender; that is, concentrating on tasks, roles, and results rather than the personality of the interviewee.[42] Ironically, by temporarily suspending intentions in performance counseling interviews, one may more likely achieve goals because interviewee resistance is decreased by curtailing judgments.[43] Feedback clarification refers to the ability to paraphrase content back to the speaker and to reflect the feelings of the speaker.[44] When an appraiser provides accurate feedback, the appraisee adds to his/her self-understanding, resulting in improved self-esteem and personal effectiveness. It is not sufficient to simply repeat back, or mimic, the words of the appraisee, it is necessary to feed back accurate understandings of both content and feelings expressed.

Much has been written about the so-called "sandwich" technique where negative evaluations are sandwiched between praises. Stano believed that skill in balancing praise and criticism in performance interviews can help circumvent the debilitating effects of evaluation; however, he believes that the "sandwich" technique is too obvious. He recommends dispensing supportive feedback almost exclusively at the beginning of the interview; thus, establishing an initial positive climate and creating appraisee receptiveness to more thorough analysis in areas where improvement is needed.[45]

Use of feedback clarification, non-evaluative listening, and balancing praise and criticism in performance interviews minimize the negative aspects of communicating evaluative messages in one other significant way: by reducing the likelihood of open hostility. Skopec's research findings support that uncertainty in dealing with confrontations and other hostile interviewee reactions and the need to maintain satisfactory interpersonal relationships following appraisal interviews constitute primary concerns of performance appraisers. When appraisees are heard accurately and understood, they are less likely to be hostile and confrontive.[46]

Laird and Clampitt claimed that the performance appraisal process may be sabotaged by multiple use of appraisal documents. Stano summarized literature on this matter and concluded that it was universally agreed that to combine discussion of development and salary is deleterious. He believed that performance interviews should have a narrow focus confined to either the objective of development or to performance/salary review.[48]   Banks and Murphy suggested that in assessing candidates for promotion, the interview should focus on behavior required for more advanced jobs, whereas in salary administration, the focus should be on behavior required in the appraisee's own job.[49]

Wexley discussed the appraisal interview in terms of two directions, administrative and employee development. The purpose of the form is to communicate and support administrative decisions such as salary increases, promotions, transfers, etc.; the purpose of the latter is to enable each employee to get feedback as to how well he/she is doing and to provide an opportunity to discuss improvement of performance. "Both (purposes) cannot usually be accomplished during the same session, inasmuch as the manager is being asked to play the conflicting roles of judge and helper."[50] Mount, in a study of employee and manager satisfaction with the appraisal process in a large corporation, found that both groups supported the concept of separating salary considerations from employee appraisals.[51] It is noteworthy that both groups consider the quality of appraisal discussion one of the most important factors is satisfaction with the program.

Combining development goals with administrative tasks such as salary administration within the appraisal interview creates an improbable communication problem in that the appraiser has dual roles. "The superior cannot establish a warm, supportive climate if he or she is ruling on the employee's paycheck. The employee will not be open to a discussion of weakness if he or she feels that such a disclosure will result in economic sanction."[52]

Every organization has a climate in which communication occurs.[53]   Climate factors must be considered at both the organizational level (macro) and at the performance appraisal interview level (micro). Climate factors at the organizational level refer to processes related to such factors as leadership, communication, decision-making, goal setting, and processes.[54] Wexley drew upon the seminal work of Likert to illustrate how organizations differ with respect to climate factors.[55] At one extreme is the System 1 organization where there is no perceived evidence of trust between manager and subordinate, interaction is restricted, decisions are all made at the top, and employee participation is discouraged. In a System 1 organization communication flows downward, tends to be distorted, inaccurate, and viewed with suspicion. At the other extreme is the System 4 organization which is characterized by supportive relationships, group decision-making, open and extensive interaction, and high participation. In a System 4 organization communication flows freely throughout-upward, downward, and laterally. Information is accurate and undistorted.[56] It is apparent that appraisal interviews would take on quite different characteristics within these different environments. What seems clear is that communication in organizations oriented toward System 4 would be quite superior to that in System 1.

Climate exists as a communication variable at the micro level of the performance appraisal interview as well. "The climate present in an appraisal interview is affected by a complexity of interlocking and intangible variables."[57] Variables include both physical and personal factors that surround the performance interview. Where the interview is held is an important factor. Experts disagree on this. Wexley suggested the interview take place in either the appraiser's or appraisee's office.[58] Stano believed the best place is a neutral territory that is relatively isolated from routine distractions.[59] What seems important is that a place be selected for the interview that is comfortable for both parties, that will provide appropriate privacy, isolation, and no interruptions, and that does not serve to increase mystery, or distance, that already exits. Arrangements within the interview room are important climate factors; those that reduce differences in status and distance facilitate effective communications. For example, side-to-side or corner seating is preferred to communicating across the expanse of a desk. Proxemic variables such as these are examples of non-verbal communication that can serve to reduce or expand status or hierarchical differences between appraiser and appraisee.

The impact of climate considerations, whether at the organizational-wide or personal level, may be observed at the appraisal interview level. If appraiser behavior is substantially incongruent with organizational characteristics experienced day-to-day by appraisees, distrust and suspicion will be engendered. If appraiser non-verbal behavior, that is, facial expression, gestures, posture, lack of eye contact, etc., contradicts what is said verbally, appraisees will get a mixed message. Non-verbal behavior is perceived as more reliable and accurate than the verbal message when they are in conflict.[60] Communicators are constantly using two channels of communication, i.e., verbal and non-verbal.

The importance of climate factors at the individual level are illustrated by Stano. "Overall, communication will be more open and honest and problem-solving will be facilitated if the manager can genuinely consider the employee as equal and can appear spontaneous, friendly, supportive, sensitive to and interested in the difficulties of the worker, understanding, and cooperative, nonjudgmental with regard to feelings revealed, nonmanipulative, concerned for the dignity and worth of the individual, trusting, and confident of the employee's abilities."[61] Figure 5.4 provides a list of factors which can constitute barriers to effective communication.

Summary

Review of the performance appraisal interview and the complex processes which occur in the act of communication between appraiser and appraisee leads to a series of statements which might summarize and give direction to communicative behavior on the part of appraisers.

1.   The appraisal interview is an exceedingly complex communication event that can have negative implications for both appraisee and appraiser. The employee may become defensive and view the interview as the deciding factor in his/her ultimate destiny. The appraiser many times experiences high levels of anxiety and feels some sense of futility in evaluating an employee's performance.

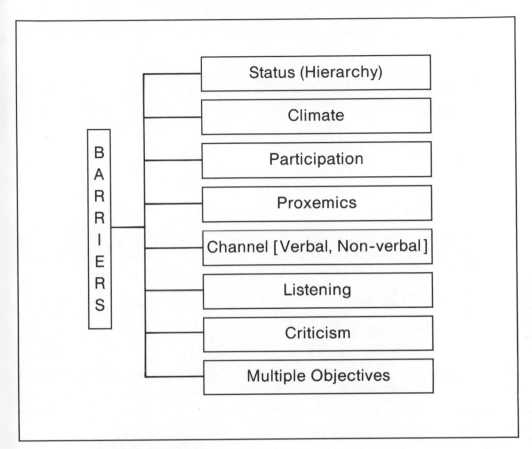

Fig. 5.4. Barriers to Effective Communication

2.   To help overcome these feelings, management should attempt to establish an environment conducive to effective communication.   Special attention should be addressed to the hierarchical nature of this communication process.

3.   Communication is a two-way process, and both parties communicating should be using the same points of reference.   Validation is accomplished through both parties providing feedback so that a common ground of understanding can be achieved.

4.   We communicate best with people who have similar backgrounds to our own and with people with whom we are neither threatened by nor do we threaten.

5.   Expectations should be made explicit and clear.

6.   Differences in beliefs cause difficulties in communication, especially in low or high self-efficacy beliefs.

7.   Differences in attitudes construct a barrier in communications between individuals.

8.   Poor listeners are not good communicators. The non-evaluative feedback rule can help open the lines of communication and assume that all the meaning intended by the sender is received by the receiver.

9.   There is a hierarchical relationship between employee and appraiser/ supervisor; i.e., there are two different classes of people, each with his/her own customs and rituals, trying to communicate but possibly not understanding where each is coming from. Thus, both may fall back on societal norms and scripts and may never actually communicate.

10.   To overcome this, a manager should facilitate participation of subordinates. This can be done through active listening, facilitative communication behaviors, and structuring the organizational and personal environment in ways that are conducive to effective communication. The purpose of the interview should be stated clearly.

11.   To reduce the negative impact of the performance interview the appraiser should provide feedback clarification, non-evaluative listening, and attempt to achieve a balance between praise and criticism.

12.   Multiple use of appraisal documents and interviews can cause problems. The interview should have precise and clearly defined parameters and not mingle personal development and administrative objectives.

13.   All organizations have a climate which consists of two levels, micro and macro; i.e., personal and organizational. Both physical and personal factors affect the climate that surrounds the performance interview. Communication will be of a higher quality in a climate which encourages participation and diminishes status differences.

14.   Finally, the sine qua non of effective performance appraisal communication is appraiser acceptance of responsibility for the quality of communication which takes place. When performance interviews are characterized by facilitative communication processes, both personal and organizational development occurs.

Endnotes

1.   Nancy K. Napier and Gary P. Latham, "Outcome Expectancies of People Who Conduct Performance Appraisals," *Personnel Psychology* 39 (Winter 1986), pp. 827-837.

2.   Robert G. Lahti, "Appraising Managerial Performance," *Junior College Resource Review*, (January 1981), pp. 3-6.

3.   Eric Wm. Skopec, "Rhetorical Dimensions of Performance Appraisal Interviews," Paper presented at the Annual Meeting of the Eastern Communication Association (75th, Philadelphia, PA, March 8-11, 1984), pp. 1-10; Napier and Latham, *op. cit.*,

pp. 827-837; and Kenneth N. Wexley, "Appraisal Interview," in *Performance Assessment: Methods and Applications*, ed. Ronald A. Berk (Baltimore: Johns Hopkins Press, 1986), pp. 167-185.

4.   Angela Laird and Phillip G. Clampitt, "Effective Performance Appraisal: Viewpoints from Managers," *The Journal of Business Communication* 22:3, pp. 49-57.

5.   H. Lloyd Goodall, Jr., Gerald L. Wilson, and Christopher L. Waagen, "The Performance Appraisal Interview: An Interpretive Assessment," *Quarterly Journal of Speech* 72 (February 1986), pp. 74-87.

6.   Skopec, *op. cit.*, pp. 1-10.

7.   Napier and Latham, *op. cit.*, pp. 827-837.

8.   Goodall, Wilson, and Waagen, *op. cit.*, p. 87.

9.   N. R. F. Meier, *Appraising Performance* (La Jolla, CA: University Associates, Inc., 1976).

10.   Norman Cousins, "The Hersey Episode," *Saturday Review* (January 1977).

11.   *Interpersonal Communication: A Guide for Staff Development*, Institute of Government, Georgia Center for Continuing Education, 1974.

12.   Mark E. Meadows, "Personal Communication and Organizational Effectiveness," *Appalachian Business Review* 7:2 (1979), pp. 2-6.

13.   Napier and Latham, *op. cit.*, pp. 827-837.

14.   Goodall, Wilson, and Waagen, *op. cit.*, pp. 74 87.

15.   Wexley, op. cit., pp. 167-185.

16.   Michael Stano, "Guidelines for Conducting the Performance Appraisal Interview: A Literature Synthesis," *Journal of Applied Communication Research* 9:2 (Fall 1981), pp. 131-142.

17.   Laird and Clampitt, *op. cit.*, pp. 49-57.

18.   Geoff Bellman, "Nine Ways to Upgrade Performance Discussions," *Training/HRD* 18 (February 1981), pp. 35-38.

19.   Wexley, *op. cit.*, pp. 167-185.

20.   Meadows, *op. cit.*, pp. 2-6.

21.   Napier and Latham, *op. cit.*, pp. 827-837.

22.   Stano, *op. cit.*, pp. 131-142.

23.   John F. Kikorski and Joseph A. Litterer, "Effective Communication in the Performance Appraisal Review," *Public Personnel Management* 12 (1983), pp. 33-42, in Goodall, Wilson, and Waagen, *op. cit.*, p. 74.

24.   Stano, *op. cit.*, pp. 131-142.

25.   Goodall, Wilson, and Waagen, *op. cit.*, pp. 74-87.

26.   Stanley B. Silverman and Kenneth N. Wexley, "Reaction of Employees to Performance Appraisal Interviews as a Function of Their Participation in Rating Scale Development," *Personnel Psychology* 37 (Winter 1984), pp. 703-710; Laird and Clampitt, *op. cit.*, pp. 49-57; Stano, *op. cit.*, pp. 131-142; and Wexley, *op. cit.*, pp. 167-185.

27.   Wexley, *op. cit.*, pp. 167-185.

28.   Kenneth Burke, *A Rhetoric of Motives* (Berkeley, CA: University of California Press, 1969) in Goodall, Wilson, and Waagen, *op. cit.*, p. 74.

29.   Goodall, Wilson, and Waagen, *op. cit.*, p. 74.

30.   *Ibid*, p. 74.

31.   *Ibid.*

32.   Stano, *op. cit.*, pp. 131-142.

33.   Goodall, Wilson, and Waagen, *op. cit.*, pp. 74-87; and Laird and Clampitt, *op. cit.*, pp. 131-142.

34.   Stano, *op. cit.*, pp. 131-142; and Goodall, Wilson, and Waagen, *op. cit.*, pp. 74-87.

35.   Goodall, Wilson, and Waagen, *op. cit.*, pp. 74-87.

36.   Stano, *op. cit.*, pp. 131-142.

37.   Goodall, Wilson, and Waagen, *op. cit.*, pp. 74-87.

38.   Bellman, *op. cit.*, pp. 35-38.

39.   Stano, *op. cit.*, pp. 131-142.

40.   Laird and Clampitt, *op. cit.*, pp. 49-57.

41.   John B. Bennett and Shirley S. Chater, "Evaluating the Performance of Tenured Faculty Members," *Educational Record* 65 (Spring 1984), pp. 38-41.

42.   Stano, *op. cit.*, pp. 131-142.

43.   Meadows, *op. cit.*, pp. 2-6.

44.   Kikorski and Litterer in Goodall, Wilson, and Waagen, *op. cit.*, p. 74.

45.   Stano, *op. cit.*, pp. 131-142.

46.   Skopec, *op. cit.*, pp. 1-10.

47.   Laird and Clampitt, *op. cit.*, pp. 49-57.

48.   Stano, *op. cit.*, pp. 131-142.

49.   Christina G. Banks and Kevin R. Murphy, "Toward Narrowing the Research-Practice Gap in Performance Appraisal," *Personnel Psychology* 38 (Summer 1985), pp. 335-345.

50.   Wexley, *op. cit.*, p. 170.

51. Michael K. Mount, "Comparisons of Managerial and Employee Satisfaction with a Performance Appraisal System," *Personnel Psychology* 36 (Spring 1983), pp. 99-109.

52. Laird and Clampitt, *op. cit.*, p. 56.

53. Meadows, *op. cit.*, pp. 2-6.

54. Wexley, *op. cit.*, pp. 167-185.

55. R. Likert, "Motivational Approach to Management Development," *Harvard Business Review* 37:4 (1959), pp. 75-82 in Stano, *op. cit.*, pp. 131-142.

56. Wexley, *op. cit.*, pp. 167-185.

57. Stano, *op. cit.*, p. 135.

58. Wexley, *op. cit.*, pp. 167-185.

59. Stano, *op. cit.*, pp. 131-142.

60. Rodney Napier and Matti K. Gersherfield, *Groups: Theory and Experience* (Boston, MA: Houghlin Mifflin Company).

61. Stano, *op. cit.*, p. 135.

6

Minimizing Rater Errors in Observing and Appraising Performance

William I. Sauser, Jr.

Having a well-designed performance appraisal instrument and process is essential if the resulting evaluations are to be useful. However, even the most carefully constructed devices and programs will not assure success in gathering valuable information if the human beings who use the instruments are not willing or able to employ them properly.

The persons who observe and appraise performance are very much a part of the measurement process. No matter how fine an instrument they are using, if the raters are unreliable or invalid in their observations and appraisals, then the resulting information will be unreliable and invalid, and thus, not suitable for any purpose.

Unfortunately, human beings tend to be very poor evaluators of behavior, as the following except from the work of John Bernardin and Richard Beatty attests:

> Research in psychology is replete with examples of the potential difficulties confronting performance appraisers. People apparently do not attend very well to base-rate information; they express excessive and unjustified confidence in their judgments; they make predictive judgments that are biased in comparison with normative standards; they are subject to hindsight biases; they have self-serving biases in person perception; they underestimate the role of contextual factors affecting behavior; their judgments of covariation are inaccurate; they resort to erroneous judgmental heuristics; and so on . . . and on. . . . There can be no question that some raters of performance commit these errors in judgment, as well as many others.[1]

The existence of these and other rater errors have been known for years.[2,3,4] Some of the more common errors which have been identified and studied in detail are described in Exhibit 6.1.[5]

Since the existence of these errors is so pervasive, and their effects are so potentially damaging, it is important to take every possible precaution to avoid them. The following ten suggestions for minimizing rater errors in observing and appraising performance are discussed in this chapter:

1. Select appropriate raters.

2. Clarify the purpose of the performance appraisal program.

3. Choose the right format and content.

4. Involve the raters in creating or interpreting the rating scale.

5. Train the raters.

6. Provide opportunities for the raters to observe the performance being appraised.

7. Help the raters keep records of meaningful observations.

8. Standardize the rating context.

9. Motivate the raters to do a good job.

10. Maintain the quality of the program.

Administrators who follow these steps when implementing their performance appraisal programs will be rewarded with more meaningful data than will those who ignore these powerful suggestions for minimizing rater errors.

1. Select appropriate raters.

There is evidence to support the belief that some persons are better than others at rating performance. For example, after reviewing numerous research studies on this topic, Ronald Taft in 1955 concluded:

> . . . that the following characteristics are fairly consistently found to be positively correlated with the ability to judge the personality characteristics of others: (a) age (children), (b) high intelligence and academic ability (with analytic judgments especially), (c) specialization in the physical sciences, (d) esthetic and dramatic interests, (e) insight into one's status with respect to one's peers on specific traits, (f) good emotional adjustment and integration . . . and (g) social skill. . . .[6]

More recently, Walter Borman found that personal qualities related to accuracy of appraisal include verbal reasoning, freedom from self-doubt, high self-control, and an orientation toward details.[7]

In most organizational settings there are practical constraints which make it difficult to apply the findings of Taft and Borman. Most administrators do not have the luxury to pick and choose accurate raters from a pool of potential appraisers. However, it would not be wise to ignore these important findings. Ratings turned in by individuals who are poorly adjusted or are undergoing a personal or emotional crisis--or who have proven to be grossly inattentive to details--are suspect and could be very damaging to the integrity of the performance appraisal process.

A more practical approach to the selection of potential raters is offered by Kenneth Wexley and Richard Klimoski. They suggest:

> The person doing the assessment must: (1) be in a position to observe the behavior and performance of the individual of interest, (2) be knowledgeable about the dimensions or features of performance, (3) have an understanding of the scale format and the instrument itself, and (4) must be motivated to do a conscientious job of rating.[8]

Note that in an academic setting this may call for multiple raters, each attending to a specific aspect of a professor's performance. For example, the department head may be in the best position to observe and evaluate adherence to policy and departmental service; students may be the best sources of data regarding the professor's day-to-day classroom performance; peers may be the best judges of the adequacy of syllabi and tests; and outside reviewers may be the best sources of unbiased evaluations of writing and creative work.

The point is that there are some steps the administrator can take to make certain that persons are fairly evaluated. Individuals who: (1) have no opportunity to observe the performance in question, (2) do not understand the rating scale, (3) are obviously biased toward or against the individual being appraised, (4) are poorly adjusted or undergoing a personal or emotional crisis, or (5) have proven to be grossly inattentive to details should not be selected to take part in the performance appraisal process.

2. Clarify the purpose of the performance appraisal program.

Performance appraisal ratings can be used for a variety of purposes, including providing feedback to the ratee, justifying personnel actions, identifying training needs and special talents, placing employees into proper jobs, fostering accountability, and improving organizational effectiveness.[9] The specific purpose for which appraisal ratings are collected can affect the motivation--and thus the behavior--of the raters who are providing the scores, as noted in the following passage from the work of Wallace Lonergan:

> Appraisal programs are doomed to failure if employees associate them with determination of firing and layoffs. Such negative associations not only engender resentment and distrust on the part of the employees, but also put the assessing supervisor on the spot. Similarly, if appraisal programs become associated with favorable management action, a supervisor, wishing to show the department in a good light, might understandably upgrade an employee's ratings, thus adding deliberate distortion to already biased human judgment.[10]

Bernardin and Beatty are also concerned that the rater have a clear understanding of the purpose of the appraisal program lest the rater distrust the process:

One factor that affects rater motivation has to do with the trust individual raters have in the appraisal process. Trust in the appraisal process may be defined as the extent to which both raters and ratees perceive that the appraisal data will be (or has been) rated accurately and fairly and the extent to which they perceive that the appraisal data will be (or has been) used fairly and objectively for pertinent personnel decisions.[11]

If the raters are confused about the purpose of the appraisal program, or if the program seems to be designed to fulfill two or more conflicting purposes, not only might the raters lose trust in the program, they may become frustrated and angry as well.

For example, suppose that one objective of an appraisal program is to determine salary increases. In this case, assessing supervisors frequently emphasize the strengths of an employee if they feel that the employee deserves an increase. Suppose that at the same time the appraisal program is being used to improve performance. With this objective in mind, the assessing supervisor may feel obligated to point out an employee's relative weaknesses in order to identify areas for improvement. Inevitably, the assessing supervisors will find themselves in a frustrating, if not untenable, position in attempting to use the assessments for these differing purposes.[12]

It was recognized at least sixty years ago that knowledge of the purpose for which ratings were to be used might influence the scores provided, therefore, the conventional wisdom was as follows: "To avoid this error, ratings should be secured with the raters in ignorance of their use and if possible at a time in advance of the situation demanding their use."[13]

Given Bernardin and Beatty's concerns about trust in the appraisal process, it is likely that this conventional wisdom could do with some revision. Administrators who desire to construct a performance appraisal system which will be accepted and used should inform the potential raters of all intended uses of the resulting data. This will at least reduce any distortion and variance in ratings due to speculation regarding their use.

As a final note, while performance appraisal ratings can indeed be used for a variety of purposes, Lonergan suggests that setting individual development as the primary objective of an appraisal program has at least four advantages:

1.   The program is likely to be more acceptable to employees and to gain their support rather than arouse their resentment.

2.   There is less obvious reason for the assessing supervisors to introduce deliberate distortion into the assessments to achieve their own ends.

3. Feelings of stress and strain on the part of both the assessing supervisors and the employees are lessened.

4. Assessments will probably reflect the facts better.[14]

3. Choose the right format and content.

As noted in Chapter Three of this volume, there is a wide variety of appraisal techniques and formats from which to choose, each with particular strengths and weaknesses.[15,16]   It does make a difference which format is chosen for use, since some formats are better suited for one use than another.

Bernardin and Beatty have provided the following summary of what they believe to be the most important contingencies regarding the efficacy of the various appraisal methods:

> If the purpose of appraisal requires comparisons of people across raters for important decisions, then Management By Objectives (MBO) . . . (is) inappropriate since (it is) typically not based on a common measurement scheme.   If there is low trust among raters, and if ratings are linked to important personnel decisions . . . , then the forced- choice method is recommended since it is more resistant to deliberate rating inflation than other methods. . . .   If the Behaviorally Anchored Rating Scale (BARS) method is to be adopted, then diary-keeping should be incorporated as a formal component of the process. . . .   Such an approach is not only more effective at inhibiting halo than other methods; it also provides documentation for summary ratings and a data source for validating individual raters.   If the purpose of appraisal is test validation, then the relatively high levels of reliability and variability for personnel-comparison methods certainly support their use, providing a behavioral format is adopted for the comparisons and assumptions can be met for comparisons across raters.   If the purpose of appraisal is to improve performance, then MBO is the best strategy, providing uncontaminated, quantifiable data are available. . . .[17]

These results of Bernardin and Beatty's comprehensive review of the research literature point out the importance of clearly defining the purpose of the performance appraisal program before choosing and implementing any particular assessment technique.

Richard Klimoski warns practitioners also to consider carefully the content of assessment before selecting a scale for implementation.   He describes three traditional options of assessment content: (1) personal traits or qualities of an individual, (2) performance results, and (3) behaviors exhibited on the job.[18]

As it turns out, each of these approaches to defining (referencing) effectiveness has strengths and weaknesses.   Each is more or less applicable to particular jobs, to types of industries, and to differing management philosophies.   Each one will be more or less appropriate depending on the purpose of the assessment. For example, a results approach might be more suitable as a basis for awarding a bonus. A behavior emphasis would be better when assessments are to be used to determine a manager's training needs. A person or trait orientation makes sense when the assessment is to be used as input to making a promotion decision. In the last case, we need to predict a person's likely future success, and knowing his or her personal traits or qualities helps us to do this.[19]

The message of this section is that the format and content of the assessment device to be implemented should certainly not be determined arbitrarily if rater errors in observation and appraisal are to be avoided. Administrators should consider carefully the organizational context, the prevailing managerial philosophy, and the purpose for carrying out the appraisal program before any decisions about format or content are made.

4. Involve the raters in creating or interpreting the rating scale.

Douglas McGregor argues that supervisors are very reluctant to "play God" in appraising employees' performance, and implies that they may intentionally distort ratings as a result of this reluctance.[20] Some of the reasons for managers' resistance to performance appraisal cited by McGregor include: (1) a normal dislike of criticizing a subordinate (and perhaps having to argue about it), (2) lack of interviewing skills, (3) dislike of new procedures with accompanying changes in ways of operating, and (4) mistrust of the validity of the appraisal instrument.[21]

Carl Kujawski and Drew Young suggest, "Too often this resistance is justified. If an appraisal program is developed independently by a staff unit and imposed from above, it has a good chance for failure. However, it doesn't have to be this way."[22]

Kujawski and Young point out Peter Drucker's major suggestion for overcoming resistance to change: "Workers must be provided with opportunities for participation that will give them a managerial view."[23] They then translate Drucker's device into a pragmatic suggestion for administrators who are trying to implement a workable appraisal program:

> One approach is to have the personnel department work with a cross section of management in developing the appraisal program. Once the outline of the program has been established, it can be circulated to a larger group of managers for review and comment, and the program modified as needed.

> Depending on the particular needs of the organization and the results desired, the number of levels of management involved in the design of the program will vary. The critical factor is that the users of the program be involved. By being so, they will come to "own" the program, and therefore will be more willing to support it because it is theirs.[24]

The motivational effect of participation in the development of performance rating scales has been documented in the research literature.[25,26] Raters are typically proud of the rating scales they develop through their own efforts and are motivated to use them effectively.

Rater participation in scale construction can also have a second major benefit, particularly when Patricia Smith and Lorne Kendall's "retranslation technique"--the process used to develop Behaviorally Anchored Rating Scales (BARS)--is employed.[27] William Sauser notes:

> When employees work together to establish a standardized set of performance levels and dimensions to evaluate, they typically reach a common understanding of the meaning of each dimension and anchor point. Thus, the rater participation process serves to greatly reduce the problem of each rater interpreting the scales differently.[28]

One problem with Smith and Kendall's retranslation process is that it is very cumbersome and time-consuming. Fortunately, a shortcut method for constructing BARS has been devised.[29,30] The psychometric quality of the scales which have been produced using this shortcut technique is similar to that of scales developed with the unabridged method.

Participation in scale construction almost always leads to an improvement in rater motivation. However, the examples described above seem to indicate that the additional benefit--creating a common understanding of the meaning of scale dimensions and anchor points--accrues only when such participation is in the form of involvement in the "retranslation process." How can this additional benefit be obtained when working with scales which are not of the BARS format?

This question has been answered by the development of a type of training program, called "frame-of-reference training," which involves raters not in the development of the scale, but rather in the interpretation of the scale.[31] An example of the practical application of frame-of-reference training is described below. In this particular example, the standardized instrument in use was a trait rating scale:

> One possible modification with which I have been experimenting in my rater training workshops may prove to be valuable. Workshop participants are asked to develop, in small task groups, meaningful definitions of each dimension of the standardized scale with which they are working. Each task group also produces behavioral anchors for each level of a particular standardized scale. After these definitions and anchors have been devised, the workshop convenes in full session, and each task group presents its products. All workshops participants then seek to agree upon a common set of performance dimensions and standards.[32]

In summary, two major benefits can result from allowing raters to participate in the scale construction or interpretation process: (1) the raters will gain a sense of "ownership" of the scale, their resistance to its use will be lessened, and the motivation to intentionally distort scale scores will be reduced; and (2) the raters are more likely to develop a common frame of reference, they will share similar interpretations of scale dimensions and anchor points, and unintentional distortion will be reduced.

Administrators wishing to minimize rater errors in observing and appraising performance would thus be well advised to allow raters to participate in the creation of the scales themselves, or at least in the interpretation of standardized scales within the organizational context.

5. Train the raters.

In 1954, J. P. Guilford stated, "Various experiences with ratings tend to show that the most effective method for improving ratings in many ways is to train raters carefully."[33] The documented effectiveness of a variety of types of training programs carried out in a number of different organizational settings in the three decades since Guilford made that statement testify to its truth.[34] In fact, Kujawski and Young claim that "A comprehensive training program for supervisors who will serve as appraisers is one of the most valuable aspects of the implementation process."[35]

What should be the content of a comprehensive rater training program? William Holley and Kenneth Jennings have supplied the following excellent answer to this question:

Training programs for appraisers should focus on improving both observational and evaluative skills. Appraisers need to be taught what kinds of behaviors distinguish high from low performers, how to avoid perceptual and judgmental errors, and how to understand appraisal formats so as to use them appropriately for their intended purposes. Also, it is important that raters know how to select the relevant information for making an accurate appraisal. Training programs should actively involve the potential appraisers in the training process, and appraisers should be provided an opportunity to participate in group discussions and practice performance interviews. While the content of the training program should vary according to the organization's needs, training should also aim to change the attitudes of the appraisers, where necessary. Frequently performance appraisal programs fail because of the lack of rater motivation either due to lack of understanding or poor instructions.[36]

Duane Schultz suggests that rater training should involve two steps:

1. Creating an awareness that abilities and skills are usually distributed in accordance with the normal curve, so that it is perfectly acceptable to find large differences among a group of workers, and

2.　　Developing the ability to define appropriate criteria for the behaviors being evaluated, a standard or average performance against which employees may be compared.[37]

James Buford and Sonya Collins add that the workshop method is an excellent way to train raters to reduce errors:

Trainees should have the opportunity to observe errors being made in an appraisal conference if possible. Videotapes are effective and can be used repeatedly. Raters should at least review written situational exercises. They should attempt to identify the errors that are being made and then complete their own ratings. Through group discussion, trainees have the opportunity to receive feedback regarding their own rating behavior and practice the correct techniques.[38]

Latham and Wexley have described in detail an excellent workshop employing the kind of videotaped exercises recommended by Buford and Collins.[39] Administrators would do well to review the Latham and Wexley program when devising their own training sessions. Another useful training device is the Atlantic Richfield Company's guide for individual raters.[40]

Exhibit 6.2 contains a detailed training outline which was devised to facilitate the implementation of a BARS-type faculty evaluation instrument in a university setting.[41] Research with this training program found it to be very effective in minimizing rater errors.[42]

The implications of this section should be very clear: Train your raters if you want to minimize errors in observing and appraising performance. Providing a comprehensive rater training program is probably the most important step in implementing an effective appraisal system. Time and energy invested in rater training will pay huge dividends in terms of the accuracy of the data resulting from the appraisal process.

6.　*Provide opportunities for the raters to observe the performance being appraised.*

In an earlier section of this chapter administrators were advised to select raters who are in a position to observe the performance in question. However, simply being in position to observe is not enough, as the following passage illustrates:

Supervisors meeting informally over coffee or lunch frequently brag about and share amusing anecdotes regarding their employees' behavior and work performance. As they do this, the supervisors are actually informally evaluating their employees, often on the basis of a few randomly observed events or remarks. . . . It is during these informal, loosely structured discussions that employees . . . begin to acquire reputations. . . . In the absence of more accurate data regarding employee work performance, . . . decisions might typically be made on the basis of the reputational factors resulting from the informal evaluation process mentioned above. However, reputations, since they are based mostly on hearsay and random comments and observations, often present inaccurate, distorted, biased pictures of employees' true abilities and performance. (I am certain that all of us from time to time wonder why our supervisors are never around to see us when we make a particularly brilliant decision or complete a difficult task, but always seem to appear just in time to catch us in a blunder.)[43]

How can an administrator make certain that a rater's observations are objective and fair rather than biased and distorted? All of the suggestions in this chapter are directed toward that end; however, there are three things in particular that should be done to address this problem.

First, the administrator should make certain that the raters understand exactly what it is they are looking for. While they are observing, they should be primed to notice specific incidents of effective or ineffective behavior. This is why a comprehensive rater training program must contain information on the kinds of behaviors which distinguish among levels of performance. As Christina Banks and Kevin Murphy state, "Training programs should not train appraisers merely to observe; rather they should train them how to decide what to observe."[44] (Note that if it is unclear what behaviors actually distinguish effective from ineffective performance, a job analysis is clearly in order.[45])

Second, the administrator should ascertain that all raters take a systematic approach to gathering the information they need to make accurate appraisals. For example, if a department head is to evaluate the quality of each faculty member's publications on an annual basis, she should certainly have a process in place to collect copies of all published work--not just those papers which the faculty happen to bring to her attention. Similarly, if a committee of peers is to evaluate a colleague's classroom teaching performance, the committee should devise and follow a plan that allows periodic classroom visits--not just a single visit that may fall on a particularly good or bad day for their colleague.

Third, the administrator should see that all raters keep some sort of orderly record of their observations. By recording these observations over a period of time, then referring to the complete record when providing an appraisal, the rater can avoid being overly influenced by recent events or isolated incidents of irregular behavior. The next section describes some of the techniques which can be employed to assist raters in keeping useful records of their observations.

7. Help the raters keep records of meaningful observations.

Many performance appraisal programs call for ratings to be collected on a periodic basis, such as annually. It is assumed that the rater takes into consideration the ratee's typical performance across the entire span of the rating period when filling out the performance appraisal form. Unfortunately, it is very difficult for supervisors to remember all of the incidents of performance which they may have observed over the year, so this assumption is very difficult to support. In fact, it is probable that many raters base their scores upon recent observations and a few "unforgettable" instances of behavior they recall from earlier in the year.

Although these recalled instances may be "unforgettable," they may not be remembered accurately, since most human beings are not blessed with total recall. Instead, these remembered samples of behavior may become distorted over time due to the frailties of human memory; they may also be colored and reinterpreted in the mind by incidents which have occurred during the intervening period of time.

Furthermore, the "unforgettable" incidents may not be typical of the ratee's day-to-day performance. While a spectacular success or failure during the year should certainly be considered when rating an employee's behavior, one or two "unforgettable" incidents should not overshadow the hundreds of instances of more typical behavior which have occurred during the rating period. Otherwise, the ratings will be distorted; they will not be valid as true measures of typical behavior across the period covered by the performance appraisal.

Since human memory is not infallible, how can raters be helped to recall accurately typical instances of behavior which occur across a span of time? The best approach is to keep records of observations as they occur, and to refer to these records when filling out the performance appraisal instrument. Three record-keeping approaches which have been devised to help raters are described in this section. These approaches are: (1) keeping a critical incident file, (2) keeping a diary, and (3) using a checklist.

In 1954, John Flanagan introduced a job analysis method which he called "the critical incident technique."[46] This method was quickly adapted for use in a performance appraisal context.[47] The method calls for the observer to provide anecdotal descriptions of effective and ineffective job behaviors which have actually been observed in the work setting. These anecdotal observations, called "critical incidents," have been characterized as follows:

> The observer reporting the critical incident is typically asked to describe:
> (1) what led up to the incident and the context in which it occurred; (2) exactly
> what the individual did that was effective or ineffective; (3) the apparent
> consequences of this behavior; and (4) whether or not the consequences were
> under the individual's control.[48]

Two examples of critical incidents, one positive and one negative, are provided in Exhibit 6.3.

During the year, the rater could jot down notes regarding all critical incidents observed, and could file these notes in a "critical incident file." This file could then be consulted when the performance appraisal form was to be completed. This procedure will ensure that behavioral observations from throughout the rating period are considered when ratings are provided, thus decreasing errors of distortion due to faulty memory.

The critical incident file will also be beneficial during counseling discussions with the ratee, since it will allow the supervisor to illustrate ratings with actual observations of behavior. This will provide more objectivity to the performance appraisal interview, and will reduce feelings of "arbitrariness" when ratings are discussed with subordinates.

Note that it is not necessary to "stockpile" the critical incident file until the annual appraisal season rolls around. Instead, each incident could serve as the basis of a contemporaneous coaching interview between the supervisor and subordinate. Positive incidents could serve as reasons for praise and other reinforcement; negative incidents as cause for correction. The critical incident file, accompanied by records of resulting commendation or reprimand, would then become a cumulative record of each subordinate's performance during the year and an objective basis for a valid performance appraisal rating.

It should be further noted that anecdotes of behavior written some time after the incidents have occurred are subject to the same errors of distortion as are other memories. It is for this reason that critical incidents should be written at the time of their occurrence, not several months later. Raters who attempt to produce from memory their critical incident files on the day they are to be used for performance appraisal purposes are negating the value of the procedure.

Flanagan's critical incident technique, combined with Smith and Kendall's application of the Thurstone scaling technique to critical incidents, has led to the development of several performance appraisal methods, including behaviorally anchored rating scales, mixed standard rating scales, and weighted checklists.[49,50] As noted earlier in this chapter, Bernardin and Beatty suggest that keeping a formal, contemporaneous diary of behavioral observations is an important component in the successful implementation of performance appraisal programs using these methods.[51] Based on their review of research regarding the usefulness of diary-keeping, they make the following recommendation:

> We recommend that a formal system of diary-keeping be implemented after rater training and that it is monitored by the rater's supervisor. We also recommend that the rater be made aware that the observation of the ratee's behavior is an important supervisory function and that the most important part of the appraisal process takes place during the observation period, rather than in the ten minutes when summary ratings are actually done.[52]

Since maintaining a critical incident file and keeping a diary are simply two different manifestations of the same concept, Bernardin and Beatty's suggestions for writing descriptions of behavior, presented in Exhibit 6.4, apply equally to both methods of record-keeping.[53]

The third technique which is available to help raters keep accurate records of their observations is the use of a checklist. Exhibit 6.5 displays a checklist devised by William Ronan for evaluating college classroom teaching effectiveness.[54]

Ronan's checklist was devised for students to use when evaluating the classroom teaching performance of their professors. Similar checklists can be devised for use by a variety of observers from different perspectives. The secret to devising these checklists is to perform a thorough job analysis--using the critical incident technique or a similar method--to determine the key behaviors which distinguish effective from ineffective performance. Brief descriptions of these key behaviors are then arranged in checklist format and provided to observers who are in a position to see the occurrence of these key behaviors.

The checklist thus serves two important purposes. It: (1) focuses the observers' attention on important behaviors, and (2) provides a record of those behaviors which were actually observed.

Note that the checklist could be formatted such that the observer would provide the actual time and place each behavior occurred, or that each incident which occurred would be described in more detail in anecdotal form. The checklist could even be formatted such that the observer could rate the frequency of occurrence of each behavior, or that each behavior be weighted in terms of its contribution to effectiveness. These and other modifications serve as the bases for such modern performance appraisal systems as Behavioral Observation Scales, Behavior Summary Scales, Behavioral Discrimination Scales, and Behavioral Assessment Approaches.[55,56]

This section has described three tools which are available to help raters keep records of meaningful observations: the critical incident file, diary-keeping, and the use of checklists. Which format is employed in any performance appraisal system is a matter of preference; however, the employment of one or more of these tools--or another such tool which forces raters to keep contemporaneous records of important instances of behavior--is essential if the system is to produce valid measures of performance during the period of time represented by the appraisal rating.

8. Standardize the rating context.

Holley and Jennings have described the importance of standardizing the performance appraisal rating process:

> Because appraisals are used to make judgments for personnel decisions, such as promotions and compensation, and appraisal data are used to make comparisons among employees, appraisal systems must be standardized in form and administration. Lack of standardization in forms, appraisers, procedures, and so on raises the question of whether differences in performance appraisals result from the system and its administration rather than from differences in employee's performance.[57]

Many of the suggestions presented in previous sections of this chapter are focused on providing this necessary standardization. For example, the proper appraisal instrument must be chosen so that all raters are using the same device. Rater selection, training, and involvement are intended to ensure that all raters share a common viewpoint and understanding of the appraisal process. The techniques described in the previous two sections are designed to make certain that there is standardization in the observation and recording of key instances of actual behavior.

However, there are other factors in the appraisal setting which also must be considered. For example, William Sauser, Carlos Arauz, and Randall Chambers found that the level of background noise present when ratings were produced could have a significant effect on those ratings.[58] Other contextual factors which have been found to influence ratings include the presence of higher-level supervisors in the room where ratings are produced, the number of ratees evaluated in one session, the presence of environmental stressors, and the time available for making the ratings.[59]

Administrators who are serious about reducing the possibility of error in performance appraisals should consider standardizing such contextual factors as the time and place in which ratings are done, the number of ratees to be appraised at one time, and the presence of supervisors, trainers, and other persons when ratings are being produced. It should be obvious that a rater who is trying to evaluate 35 subordinates in an hour while working in a hot, crowded, noisy room late at night will quite likely produce different scores than when evaluating five subordinates in an entire morning while working in quiet, comfortable surroundings.

To maintain fairness for all ratees, the administrator should ascertain that all ratings are produced under the same standardized environmental conditions. This may require, for instance, that a specified time and place be established at which all raters will perform their work.

9. *Motivate the raters to do a good job.*

No matter how sophisticated a performance appraisal system has been established, no matter how well the raters have been trained, no matter how many observations of behavior have been recorded, no matter how carefully the context has been standardized, there still remains an essential factor which heavily influences the validity of the ratings obtained: "individual raters and their motivation (or lack of motivation) to rate accurately."[60]

Richard Klimoski makes the following observation concerning this crucial factor:

(Ultimately) the critical issue of motivation toward accuracy must be confronted. But, in my opinion, it can only be dealt with by creating a climate or ethic for careful and considered employee assessment. I also feel that prime responsibility for doing this lies with upper management, and especially with the chief executive officer.[61]

Some of the ideas Klimoski provides to create this climate include the following:

1. Top management must establish and support specialists within the organization itself who are capable of developing and implementing appraisal systems.

2. Top management must personally use and demonstrate careful assessment of its own staff. Actions speak louder than words.

3. Careful performance assessment should be made an explicit part of each manager's job responsibility. It may even be written into a job description.

4. Make use of appraisal data in corporate decisions affecting staffing. . . . Decisions with regard to promotions, to reductions in force, or to salary adjustments should be based, at least in part, on assessed performance.[62]

Commitment from the top has long been recognized as the key to successful implementation of any organization-wide program. Klimoski has provided excellent advice to be followed by administrators who want to demonstrate a real commitment to the implementation of a valid performance appraisal system.

10. Maintain the quality of the program.

Any administrator who follows the nine suggestions described above when developing and implementing a performance appraisal program will most likely construct an outstanding system which will produce valid, useful results. However, just like the finest automobiles, performance appraisal systems must be properly maintained if they are to continue to operate at optimal levels.

The administrator who wishes to maintain an excellent system should make certain that appraisal forms and observational aids are kept relevant and up-to-date, particularly when job content has changed. New supervisors must be properly trained, and all raters should be given periodic "refresher courses" to make certain they are continuing to interpret and use the scales in the prescribed manner. Statistical analyses should be performed to monitor the reliability and validity of performance appraisal ratings.[63] Raters should be periodically reminded of the importance of accurate ratings, and reinforced for doing a good job of appraising and developing subordinates. Finally, the entire appraisal process should be subjected to a periodic program evaluation to make certain that it is still meeting the objectives originally established for it--and revised if it is not, or if the objectives have changed.

Within this context of program evaluation for performance appraisal systems, the administrator should attend to the sage words of Kujawski and Young:

Ensuring that the appraisal forms are being completed is only part of the monitoring procedure. Many organizations are proud of the fact that all of their appraisal forms are submitted on time with all of the proper signatures in their proper places and that they have files full of them to prove that this is being done. But how well are the appraisals being used? In an effective program, the emphasis is on the results produced. These can be checked by asking such questions as: What is the turnover rate? Are people being promoted from within or does the organization have to go outside to get qualified people to fill vacancies? How do the people using the program feel about it? Do they feel that it is meeting their needs and the needs of the organization? Is it being revised to meet changing organizational goals?[64]

After all, the performance appraisal system is a tool designed to enhance organizational effectiveness. It should be examine periodically to make certain that it is achieving that purpose.

Conclusion

Due to the frailties of human skills in observation, perception, memory, and evaluation, any performance appraisal system which includes human beings as part of the process will necessarily include some level of error. However, there are steps which administrators can take to greatly minimize this level of error.

This chapter has presented ten techniques which are designed to reduce rater errors in observing and appraising performance. These techniques are: (1) select appropriate raters, (2) clarify the purpose of the performance appraisal program, (3) choose the right format and content, (4) involve raters in creating or interpreting the rating scale, (5) train the raters, (6) provide opportunities for the raters to observe the performance being appraised, (7) help the raters keep records of meaningful observations, (8) standardize the rating context, (9) motivate the raters to do a good job, and (10) maintain the quality of the program.

Administrators who use these techniques when devising and implementing their performance appraisal programs will be richly rewarded. The resulting appraisal systems should serve as powerful tools for enhancing organizational effectiveness.

Endnotes

1.   H. John Bernardin and Richard W. Beatty, *Performance Appraisal: Assessing Human Behavior at Work*, (Boston: Kent, 1984), pp. 238-239.

2.   J. P. Gilford, *Psychometric Methods* 2nd ed., (New York: McGraw-Hill, 1954), pp. 278-280.

3.   William I. Sauser, Jr., *A Comparative Evaluation of the Effects of Rater Participation and Rater Training on Characteristics of Employee Performance Appraisal Ratings and Related Mediating Variables (Doctoral Dissertation), (Atlanta: Georgia Institute of Technology, 1978), pp. 16-20.*

4.   Patricia C. Smith, "The Problem of Criteria," in *Handbook of Industrial and Organizational Psychology*, ed. Marvin D. Dunnette (Chicago: Rand McNally, 1976), pp. 757-758.

5.   Adapted from Sauser, *A Comparative Evaluation*, pp. 216-217.

6.   Ronald Taft, "The Ability to Judge People," *Psychological Bulletin* 52 (January 1955), p. 20

7.   Walter C. Borman, "Individual Differences Correlates of Accuracy in Evaluating Others' Performance Effectiveness," *Applied Psychological Measurement* 3 (Winter 1979), pp. 103-115.

8.   Kenneth N. Wexley and Richard Klimoski, "Performance Appraisal: An Update," in *Managing Human Resources in Retail Organizations*, ed. Arthur P. Brief (Lexington, MA: Lexington Books, 1984), p. 84.

9.   William I. Sauser, Jr., "Evaluating Employee Performance: Needs, Problems, and Possible Solutions," *Public Personnel Management* 9 (January-February 1980), pp. 11-18.

10.   Wallace G. Lonergan, "Appraisal, Performance," in *Handbook for Professional Managers*, eds. Lester R. Bittell and Jackson E. Ramsey (New York: McGraw-Hill, 1985), p. 33.

11.   Bernardin and Beatty, *op. cit.*, p. 268.

12.   Lonergan, *op. cit.*, p. 33.

13.   Guilford, *op. cit.*, p. 295.

14.   Lonergan, *op. cit.*, p. 33.

15.   Bernardin and Beatty, *op. cit.*, pp. 62-127.

16.   Carl J. Kujawski and Drew M. Young, "Appraisals of 'People' Resources," in *ASPA Handbook of Personnel and Industrial Relations*, eds. Dale Yoder and Herbert G. Heneman, Jr. (Washington, DC: Bureau of National Affairs, 1979), pp. 4.185-4.199.

17.   Bernardin and Beatty, *op. cit.*, pp. 233-234.

18.   Richard Klimoski, "Performance Assessment and Retail Organizational Effectiveness," in *Managing Human Resources in Retail Organizations*, ed. Arthur P. Brief (Lexington, MA: Lexington Books, 1984), pp. 68-69.

19.   Klimoski, *op. cit.*, p. 69.

20.   Douglas McGregor, *The Human Side of Enterprise*, (New York: McGraw-Hill, 1960).

21.   Douglas McGregor, "An Uneasy Look at Performance Appraisal," *Harvard Business Review* 35 (May-June 1957), pp. 89-94.

22.   Kujawski and Young, *op. cit.*, pp. 4.163-4.164.

23.   Peter Drucker, *The Practice of Management*, (New York: Harper and Row, 1954), p. 303.

24.   Kujawski and Young, *op. cit*, p. 4.164.

25.   Sauser, *A Comparative Evaluation*.

26.   Stanley B. Silverman and Kenneth N. Wexley, "Reaction of Employees to Performance Appraisal Interviews as a Function of Their Participation in Rating Scale Development," *Personnel Psychology* 37 (Winter 1984), pp. 703-710.

27.   Patricia C. Smith and Lorne M. Kendall, "Retranslation of Expectations: An Approach to the Construction of Unambiguous Anchors for Rating Scales," *Journal of Applied Psychology* 47 (February 1963), pp. 149-155.

28.   Sauser, "Evaluating Employee Performance," p. 16.

29.   Samuel B. Green, William I. Sauser, Jr., James N. Fagg, and Cecilia H. Champion, "Shortcut Methods for Deriving Behaviorally Anchored Rating Scales," *Educational and Psychological Measurement* 41 (Fall 1981), pp. 761-775.

30.   Cecilia H. Champion, Samuel B. Green, and William I. Sauser, Jr., "Development and Evaluation of Shortcut-Derived Behaviorally Anchored Rating Scales," *Educational and Psychological Measurement* 48 (Spring 1988), pp. 29-41.

31.   Bernardin and Beatty, *op. cit.*, pp. 258-262.

32.   Sauser, *op. cit.*, p. 16.

33.   Guilford, *op. cit.*, p. 280.

34.   Sauser, *A Comparative Evaluation*, pp. 39-43.

35.   Kujawski and Young, *op. cit.*, p. 4.165.

36.   William H. Holley and Kenneth M. Jennings, *Personnel/Human Resource Management: Contributions and Activities* 2nd ed., (Chicago: Dryden 1987), p. 272.

37.   Duane P. Schultz, *Psychology and Industry Today* 3rd ed., (New York: Macmillan, 1982), p. 181.

38.   James A. Buford, Jr. and Sonya T. Collins, *Performance Appraisal: Concepts and Techniques for Local Government*, (Auburn University, AL: Alabama Cooperative Extension Service, 1986), p. 37.

39.   Gary P. Latham and Kenneth N. Wexley, *Increasing Productivity Through Performance Appraisal*, (Reading, MA: Addison-Wesley, 1981), pp. 107-111.

40.   Kujawski and Young, *op. cit.*, pp. 4.182-4.184.

41.   Sauser, *op. cit.*, pp. 212-218.

42.   *Ibid.*

43. Sauser, "Evaluating Employee Performance," p. 11.

44. Christina G. Banks and Kevin R. Murphy, "Toward Narrowing the Research-Practice Gap in Performance Appraisal," *Personnel Psychology* 38 (Summer 1985), p. 341.

45. Ernest J. McCormick, "Job and Task Analysis," in *Handbook of Industrial and Organizational Psychology*, ed. Marvin D. Dunnette (Chicago: Rand McNally, 1976).

46. John C. Flanagan, "The Critical Incident Technique," *Psychological Bulletin* 51 (July 1954), pp. 327-358.

47. John C. Flanagan and Robert K. Burns, "The Employee Performance Record: A New Appraisal and Development Tool," *Harvard Business Review* 33 (September 1955), pp. 95-102.

48. William I. Sauser, Jr., "Critical Incident Technique," in *Concise Encyclopedia of Psychology*, ed. Raymond J. Corsini (New York: Wiley, 1987), p. 272.

49. Smith and Kendall, *op. cit.*

50. Sauser, *op. cit.*

51. Bernardin and Beatty, *op. cit.*, p. 233.

52. Ibid., pp. *262-264*.

53. *Ibid.*, pp. 263-264.

54. William W. Ronan, *Evaluating College Classroom Teaching Effectiveness* (PREP Report No. 34), (Washington, DC: U.S. Government Printing Office, 1972), pp. 23-25.

55. Wexley and Klimoski, *op. cit.*, p. 81.

56. Latham and Wexley, *op. cit.*

57. Holley and Jennings, *op. cit.*, p. 271.

58. William I. Sauser, Jr., Caros G. Arauz, and Randall M. Chambers, "Exploring the Relationship Between Level of Office Noise and Salary Recommendations: A Preliminary Research Note," *Journal of Management* 4 (Spring 1978), pp. 57-63.

59. Sauser, *A Comparative Evaluation*, p. 32.

60. Bernardin and Beatty, *op. cit.*, pp. 267-268.

61. Klimoski, *op. cit.*, p. 72.

62. *Ibid.*

63. Guilford, *op. cit.*, pp. 373-413.

64. Kujawski and Young, *op. cit.*, p. 4.167.

Exhibit 6.1. Common Rater Errors Which Should Be Avoided

Leniency -- This error occurs when the supervisor rates an employee (and probably other employees) higher on every item of the rating scale than the employee's true level of performance actually deserves.

Severity -- This error, the opposite of leniency, occurs when the supervisor rates an employee (and probably other employees) lower on every item of the rating scale than the employee's true level of performance actually deserves.

Central Tendency -- This error occurs when the evaluator uses only the central portion of the scale, ignoring the high and low extremes, even when the employee's true level of performance deserves an unusually high or low rating.

Extremity -- This error, the opposite of central tendency, occurs when the evaluator uses only the high and low extremes of the scale, ignoring the central portion, even when the employee's true level of performance deserves a more moderate rating.

Halo -- This error occurs when the evaluator forms a general, overall impression of the employee's performance, then fills out the rating form to reflect this impression. This practice should be avoided. Instead, the rater should consider each item on the scale individually and should try not to let his/her rating of the employee on one item influence the rating on another item.

Logical -- This error, similar to the halo error, occurs when the evaluator, in an attempt to appear consistent, bases his/her rating on "logic" rather than on observation, thus allowing his/her response to one scale item to unjustly influence the response to another. As stated above, each item on the scale should be considered individually. An employee's level of performance will typically not be perfectly consistent (from item to item), thus there is no requirement that the rating of the employee be somehow logically consistent. What is important is that the ratings reflect only the employee's actual level of performance on each item.

Proximity -- This error, similar to the two above, occurs when the supervisor allows his/her rating on one item of the scale to influence the rating on a second item simply because the two items are located close to one another on the scale. Again, each item should be considered independently.

Contrast and Comparison -- These errors occur when the supervisor rates his/her employees *not* according to the standards specified on the scale, but in contrast or comparison to some other kind of standard, such as the performance of the best or worst employee the supervisor has ever known, the level of performance the supervisor thinks he/she could attain if he/she were doing the job, etc. Each employee should be evaluated independently according to the standards specified on the rating scale, *not* in comparison with other employees, ideals, etc.

Source: William I. Sauser, Jr., *A Comparative Evaluation of the Effects of Rater Participation and Rater Training on Characteristics of Employee Performance Appraisal Ratings and Related Mediating Variables* (Doctoral Dissertation) (Atlanta: Georgia Institute of Technology, 1978), pp. 216-217.

Exhibit 6.2. A Comprehensive Training Outline for Student Raters of Faculty Classroom Teaching Performance

I. Clarification of the aims and purposes of rating.

    A. The evaluation of professors' teaching performance is a commonly occurring event.

        1. When we think of "faculty evaluation," we usually visualize a formal process involving rating forms, computer printouts, etc. Actually, the evaluation of professors' teaching performance occurs quite often, usually in an informal manner.

        2. Students frequently "compare notes" and "spread the word" about professors. As they do this, the students are informally evaluating their professors, often on the basis of reputation and randomly observed events.

        3. Professors often evaluate themselves and other professors in informal discussions. These informal evaluations also may be largely based on reputation and randomly observed events, as well as comments from two or three students.

        4. Deans, department heads, and others are faced with making decisions regarding promotion, tenure, salary, course assignments, etc., for their professors. These decisions require some type of evaluation of the professors in question. When objective data are not available, these decisions are frequently based upon some type of informal evaluation, such as reputation, random observations, or the comments of two or three students or faculty members, even though these are certainly not the fairest ways to evaluate faculty members.

    B. There is a need for systematic, objective information regarding teaching performance.

        1. For lack of more objective data, important decisions are often made on the basis of the "informal evaluation" described above. As noted, much of this informal evaluation is based on hearsay, reputation, random comments and observations, etc. These sources are often inaccurate and even unfair. They typically present a distorted, biased picture of the professor's true teaching ability and performance. In order to increase the possibilities of appropriate, unbiased, fair decisions being made, it is necessary to gather more objective, systematic, relevant information about faculty teaching performance. Teacher rating forms are one means of making faculty evaluation more objective and systematic, and less biased.

        2. One major problem with many faculty rating forms is that they can be interpreted differently by each student rater. Thus, characteristics of the type of form used can influence the outcome of a teacher evaluation project. Students do not always agree on the definition of "good teaching performance," and what one sees as "excellent" performance may be only "fair" to another. Since the outcome of the rating process can be as easily influenced by how the raters interpret the form as by the faculty member's actual teaching performance, it is important to make sure that all of the raters interpret the form as similarly as possible. The teaching behaviors to be evaluated and the meaning of each point on the scale should be clearly specified to ensure nearly uniform interpretation. Otherwise, the raters may all be rating different aspects of behavior, and the data will not be meaningful.

        3. In order to be useful, faculty evaluation data must be reliable. That is, the evaluations by several independent raters of the same professor's teaching performance in the same class should be relatively consistent--there should be relatively high agreement among the raters. If there is a very low rate of agreement among the raters, the information will obviously be of little use.

C. Some uses of objective faculty evaluation data.

1. *Feedback*--Objective faculty evaluation data serve as relatively effective feedback from the students to their professors. Teacher evaluation forms enable students to communicate ideas to their teachers, to make their teachers aware of particular strengths and weaknesses in their courses and in their teaching methods, and to suggest improvement when necessary. Since learning depends on feedback, this information is essential if professors are to improve their courses and teaching methods in the future. The primary use of faculty rating forms is to provide this important feedback to the individual faculty members.

2. *Personnel actions*--Objective faculty evaluation data, when available, can be used to influence decisions regarding such issues as tenure, promotion, and salary adjustment. Decisions based on objective data are typically fairer than those based on hearsay, reputation, and other "informal" data. Student evaluations of teaching performance are rarely the major criteria considered when personnel action decisions are made, but they can certainly have some influence.

3. *Development*--Objective faculty evaluation data can help deans and department heads identify any particular training needs or special talents in their professors, thus providing them with suggestions for faculty development. Individual professors can also identify their own particular weaknesses and seek to improve themselves.

4. *Placement*--Objective faculty evaluation data can be used to influence decisions regarding course assignments, class sizes, etc.

5. *Responsibility*--The faculty evaluation process often enhances a professor's feelings of responsibility toward his/her students and duties as a teacher.

6. *Effectiveness*--Through the above uses, objective faculty evaluation data can help improve departmental, school, and university effectiveness, as well as the effectiveness of the individual faculty member.

D. Additional points regarding faculty evaluation.

1. There are many different duties involved in the job of college professor. While classroom teaching is not the professor's only responsibility, it *is* an important part of his/her job. Auburn University lists teaching as its faculty members' most important duty.

2. Students are not the only persons whose evaluations of teaching performance should be sought, but their evaluations should be considered carefully. Students are one of the major consumer groups of the university's expertise and are certainly affected by the faculty's performance. Furthermore, whereas deans, department heads, and other faculty members rarely observe professors' teaching performance first-hand, and thus are not in a strong position to provide objective data, students are in an excellent position to observe and report on faculty teaching behavior.

3. Teaching is multi-dimensional. There are many facets of teaching performance and it is probably not possible to take all of them into account in any one performance measure or rating form. The rating form should, however, cover as many important teaching behaviors as possible and should certainly provide adequate coverage of the facets it is intended to measure.

4. The purpose of faculty evaluation is to improve professors' teaching performance, *not* to damage faculty members in any way. The process should only be used constructively, never destructively.

II.   Introduction of the Behaviorally Anchored Rating Scale.

A.   Most faculty rating forms are developed by administrators or faculty committees with limited student input. The scale used in this project, however, was developed through student participation, and is intended to be clear and meaningful to student raters. The scale dimensions and behavioral examples were provided by Auburn students participating in earlier phases of this study.

(Note: At this point in the training session the scale is shown to the trainees. A full description of the scale includes the following points.)

B.   Instruction on the meaning of the characteristics to be evaluated.

C.   Instruction on the meaning of each anchor point used on the scale.

D.   Instruction on how to use the scale.

III.   Instruction on the avoidance of common pitfalls in rating.

A.   Lack of objectivity.

1.   Some student raters evaluate their professors on the basis of supposition, guesswork, and reputation, thus defeating the entire purpose of using the rating forms. A student's rating of his/her professor should be based only upon first-hand observations of actual behaviors, not comments made by other students, reputational factors, etc. A student who has not observed a teacher first-hand should not evaluate that teacher. Nor should a student let his/her rating of a professor be influenced by what other students think.

2.   Some student raters base their entire rating of a professor on one or two instances of extremely good or extremely poor teaching behavior. While these isolated extreme instances should certainly be considered, it is important also to keep in mind the typi-cal, "day-in, day-out" behavior of the professor.

3.   All students tend to have "first impressions" of their teachers, but some students never change these impressions, even in the face of behaviors to the contrary, and base their ratings exclusively on their first impressions. The professor's behavior throughout the quarter should be considered when his/her performance is being evaluated.

4.   The most common problem involving lack of objectivity is allowing some biasing factor to affect a professor's rating. As difficult as it is, student raters should strive not to let such factors as the professor's age, sex, rank, or appearance, the course's level of difficulty, or the student's own performance (i.e., grade in the course) or personal liking or disliking of the professor influence the performance ratings given to the professor. A student's rating of his/her professor should be influenced *only* by the professor's actual behavior while teaching the course, *not* by any biasing factor. Non-teaching behaviors, such as consulting and research, should also typically be ignored when the professor's *teaching* performance is being evaluated.

B.   Common rating "errors" to avoid.

(Note: This presentation is accompanied by a visual display of how these errors would appear on the Behaviorally Anchored Rating Scale.)

1.   *Leniency*--This "error" occurs when the student rates the professor (and probably other professors) higher on every item of the rating scale than the professor's true level of performance actually deserves.

2. *Severity*--This "error," the opposite of leniency, occurs when the student rates the professor (and probably other professors) lower on every item of the rating scale than the professor's true level of performance actually deserves.

3. *Central tendency*--This "error" occurs when the student uses only the central portion of the scale, ignoring the high and low extremes, even when the professor's true level of performance deserves an unusually high or low rating.

4. *Extremity*--This "error," the opposite of central tendency, occurs when the student uses only the high and low extremes of the scale, ignoring the central portion, even when the professor's true level of performance deserves a more moderate rating.

5. *Halo*--This "error" occurs when the student forms a general, overall impression of the professor's performance, then fills out the rating form to reflect this impression. This practice should be avoided. Instead, the student rater should consider each item on the scale individually, and should try not to let his/her rating of the teacher on one item influence the rating on another item.

6. *Logical*--This "error," similar to the "halo error," occurs when the student, in an attempt to appear consistent, bases his/her rating on "logic" rather than observation, thus allowing his/her response to one scale item to unjustly influence the response to another. As stated above, each item on the scale should be considered individually. A professor's level of performance will typically not be perfectly consistent (from item to item), thus there is no requirement that the student's rating of the professor be some-how logically consistent. What is important is that the ratings reflect only the professor's actual level of performance on each item.

7. *Proximity*--This "error," similar to the two above, occurs when the student allows his/her rating on one item of the scale to influence the rating on a second item simply because the two items are located close to one another on the scale. Again, each item should be considered independently.

8. *Contrast and comparison*--These "errors" occur when the student rates his professor *not* according to the standards specified on the scale, but in contrast or comparison to some other kind of standard, such as the performance of the best or worst professor the student has even known, the level of performance the student thinks he/she could attain if he/she were teaching the course, etc. Each professor should be evaluated independently according to the standards specified on the rating scale, *not* in comparison with other teachers, ideals, etc.

IV. Practice in the use of scales.

(Note: During the time remaining in the training session, students practice using the Behaviorally Anchored Rating Scales to evaluate professors of their own choosing. [No professors are identified.] Students are encouraged to examine their own ratings for examples of bias and error, and to correct their ratings when appropriate.)

Source: William I. Sauser, Jr., *A Comparative Evaluation of the Effects of Rater Participation and Rater Training on Characteristics of Employee Performance Appraisal Ratings and Related Mediating Variables* (Doctoral Dissertation) (Atlanta: Georgia Institute of Technology, 1978), pp. 212-218.

Exhibit 6.3.   Examples of Positive and Negative Incidents of College Classroom Teaching Behavior

Example A (Positive): On the first day of his class, Professor Jones passed out a detailed syllabus which included his office location, hours, and telephone number; a description of the textbook and daily reading assignments; his objectives for the course; his policies on attendance, testing, calculation of grades, and dishonest behavior; and descriptions of several required class assignments. He discussed the syllabus in class and answered all questions asked about it. The syllabus served as "the rules of the class," and any questions about grading, attendance, or assignments which came up during the semester were answered with reference to the written syllabus. The students reported that they appreciated having the professor's policies set out clearly at the beginning of the semester so that they knew exactly what was expected of them. They reported that the syllabus created a sense of fairness and allowed them to concentrate their attention on learning course content rather than trying to figure out what was expected of them by Professor Jones.

Example B (Negative): Following a lecture over a very complex theory, Professor Smith asked his students if they had any questions. One student, obviously confused, asked a question which revealed his lack of understanding of the theory. Professor Smith "blew up" at the student and called him "a stupid idiot" for failing to understand the theory. Professor Smith did not answer the question, nor were any other questions asked by the students. After class, several of his classmates told the student who had asked the question that they had not understood the theory either, but had been to afraid to ask a question lest they too be humbled in class. Several students failed the subsequent test because their answers indicated a lack of understanding of the theory. By handling the student's question differently, Professor Smith might have been able to better educate these students.

Exhibit 6.4. Bernardin and Beatty's Suggestions for Writing Descriptions of Behavior

1.   Use specific examples of behavior, not *conclusions* about the "goodness" or "badness" of behavior.

   Use this: Gwen told her secretary when the work was to be completed, whether it was to be a draft or a final copy, the amount of space in which it had to be typed, and the kind of paper necessary.

   Not this: Liesa gives good instructions to her secretary. Her instructions are clear and concise.

2.   Avoid using *adjective qualifiers* in the statements; use descriptions of behavior.

   Use this: Aimee repeated an employee's communication and its intent to the employee. She talked in private, and I have never heard her repeat the conversation to others.

   Not this: Kelly does a good job of understanding problems. She is kind and friendly.

3.   Avoid using statements that make *assumptions* about an employee's *knowledge* of the job; use descriptions of behavior.

   Use this: Sarah performed the disassembly procedure for rebuilding a carburetor by first removing the cap and then proceeding with the internal components. When she was in doubt about the procedure, she referred to the appropriate manual.

   Not this: Sam knows how to disassemble a carburetor in an efficient and effective manner.

4.   Avoid using *frequencies* in statements; use descriptions of behavior.

   Use this: Patrol Officer Garcia performed the search procedure by first informing the arrested of their rights, asking them to assume the search position, and then conducting the search by touching the arrested in the prescribed places. When the search was completed, Garcia informed the arrested. He then proceeded to the next step in the arrest procedure.

   Not this: Patrol Officer Dzidzo always does a good job in performing the search procedure.

5.   Avoid using *quantitative values* (numbers); use descriptions of behavior.

   Use this: Nancy submitted her reports on time. They contained no misinformation or mistakes. When discrepancies occurred on reports from the last period, she identified the causes by referring to the changes in accounting procedures and the impact they had on this period.

   Not this: Mr. Boebel met 90% of deadlines with 95% accuracy.

6.   Provide sufficient detail so that an assessment can be made of the extent to which characteristics of the situation beyond the control of the ratee may have affected the behavior.

   Use this: Mr. Dzaidzo's failure to hit the "target date" for the sky-hook quota was caused by the failure of Mr. Ressler's department to provide the ordered supply of linkage gaskets. Mr. Dzaidzo submitted four memos in anticipation of and in reference to the gasket shortage.

   Not this: It wasn't Dzaidzo's fault that he didn't hit the deadline.

Source: From H. John Bernardin and Richard W. Beatty, Performance Appraisal: Assessing Human Behaviour at Work (Boston: Kent Publishing Company, 1984) pp. 263-4. © by Wadsworth, Inc. Reprinted by permission of PWS-KENT Publishing Company, a division of Wadsworth, Inc.

Exhibit 6.5. Ronan's Evaluative Questions for Assessing Teaching Performance

Note: Each section would be headed with a question such as "Did the professor in this course . . .?"

I.   **Personal Relationships with Students**   Yes   No

1.   Know or attempt to know students' names?   ____   ____
2.   Talk with students before and/or after class?   ____   ____
3.   Hold social events for his students?   ____   ____
4.   Give advice or assistance at student request (class or office)
     with personal problems?   ____   ____
5.   Discuss (answer questions on) extra class issues?   ____   ____
6.   Compliment students on good answers?   ____   ____
7.   Encourage (answer) all questions in class?   ____   ____
8.   Treat all students equally (regardless of sex, major, etc.)?   ____   ____
9.   Ridicule, "ride," or otherwise embarrass students (either on questions or
     their performance)?   ____   ____
10. Encourage or give individual help with course material (class or office)? ____   ____
11. Lose control of himself in class (shout, curse, show anger, etc.)? ____   ____
12. Bother (harass) students during recitation, quizzes, etc.?   ____   ____
13. Make threats concerning classwork or personal behavior?   ____   ____
14. Accept legitimate excuses, explanations (as for missing quiz)?   ____   ____
15. Refuse to listen to or recognize other viewpoints in class?   ____   ____
16. Say or indicate in some way that students are inferior?   ____   ____
17. Provide special "help" sessions for course material (individual and/or class)? ____   ____

II.   **Classroom Administration**

1.   Meet all scheduled (rescheduled) classes?   ____   ____
2.   Arrive on time for all classes?   ____   ____
3.   Inform class if he would be absent?   ____   ____
4.   Discuss quiz dates or deadlines for student convenience?   ____   ____
5.   End lectures at end of classtime?   ____   ____
6.   Distribute a course outline or study plan (course objectives)?   ____   ____
7.   Follow course outline or study plan?   ____   ____
8.   Give examples of quiz items?   ____   ____
9.   Require and grade homework?   ____   ____
10. Return papers and quizzes promptly?   ____   ____
11. Permit classroom disturbances (such as students talking to each other)? ____   ____
12. Make false statements concerning course requirements (number of
     cuts, grading, etc.)?   ____   ____
13. Give excessive work?   ____   ____

III. Student Participation

Yes   No

1. Ask student preference as to topics covered?
2. Ask students to critique his teaching? ___ ___
3. Schedule quizzes, deadlines, etc., at the convenience of the class majority? ___ ___
4. Encourage (ask for) discussion, questions, or student opinions? ___ ___
5. Ask questions to determine class (individual) understanding of course material? ___ ___

IV. Classroom Presence

1. Appear well groomed?
2. Speak clearly and distinctly: ___ ___
   a. Mumble?
   b. Talk too softly? ___ ___
   c. Talk in a monotone? ___ ___
3. Use dramatic gestures (phrases) to emphasize important points? ___ ___
4. Use humor in lecture to illustrate points? ___ ___
5. Read lectures from notes or book? ___ ___
6. Appear nervous, ill-at-ease during lecture? ___ ___
7. Talk or present material too rapidly? ___ ___
8. Give rambling, disorganized lecture? ___ ___
9. Look at students during lecture? ___ ___
10. Use language students understand? ___ ___
11. Use profane language excessively? ___ ___

V. Organization and Presentation of Material

1. Begin class with a review of previous work?
2. Stress, in some way, important points in the material? ___ ___
3. Use current, pertinent, and/or personal examples to illustrate point? ___ ___
4. Show usefulness of material in "real world"? ___ ___
5. Admit not knowing answer to a question? ___ ___
6. Use outside references to supplement course? ___ ___
7. Distribute handouts/notes to supplement course? ___ ___
8. Use visual aids to supplement lecture? ___ ___
9. Provide for field trips? ___ ___
10. Have guest lecturers? ___ ___
11. Have full command of the subject matter? ___ ___
12. Give lectures different from (supplement) text? ___ ___
13. Cover all course requirements? ___ ___
14. Avoid trivial detail? ___ ___
15. Answer questions; work problems if requested? ___ ___
16. Lecture over students' heads? ___ ___
17. Give erroneous information about course material? ___ ___
18. Refuse to explain material? ___ ___
19. Make students learn "on-their-own"? ___ ___
20. Follow course schedule? ___ ___
21. Prepare for class? ___ ___

VI.   **Evaluation of Student Performance**   Yes   No

   1.   Base tests on relevant (covered) material?   ____   ____
   2.   Base tests on knowledge or principles rather than memorization?   ____   ____
   3.   Base tests on emphasized material?   ____   ____
   4.   Make tests too easy or difficult?   ____   ____
   5.   Schedule quizzes at regular intervals?   ____   ____
   6.   Allow adequate time to complete tests?   ____   ____
   7.   Comment on (correct) returned papers, quizzes, etc.?   ____   ____
   8.   Excuse high average students from final?   ____   ____
   9.   Permit extra work to improve grade?   ____   ____
  10.   Disregard lowest test score in grading?   ____   ____
  11.   Use same tests every quarter?   ____   ____
  12.   Refuse to explain grading system?*   ____   ____
  13.   Tell how students are to be graded?   ____   ____
  14.   Curve grades either:
      a. To compare individual performance with class performance?   ____   ____
      b. To reduce student grades?   ____   ____
  15.   Return all papers and quizzes?   ____   ____
  16.   Grade all quizzes and assignments?   ____   ____
  17.   Give makeup tests at individual convenience?   ____   ____
  18.   Grade on such things as major, sex, athlete, etc.?*   ____   ____
  19.   Grade on class attendance?*   ____   ____
  20.   Give final grades in accord with test scores?*   ____   ____
  21.   Grade on final exam only?   ____   ____
  22.   Pass/fail a predetermined percentage of the class?   ____   ____
  23.   Try to have makeup tests excessively difficult?   ____   ____
  24.   Change a clearly unfair grade?*   ____   ____
  25.   Consider effort, participation, application in assigning final grade?   ____   ____
  26.   Use student to grade work?   ____   ____

VII.   **Interest in Job of Teaching**

   1.   Make derogatory comments about teaching?   ____   ____
   2.   Make derogatory comments about the course?   ____   ____
   3.   Indicate he would rather consult and/or do research than teach?   ____   ____
   4.   Criticize fellow teachers?   ____   ____

*This item would have to be answered after the student received his final grade. The major difficulty here would be administrative, that is, submitting the question to students after the course is over and having it returned. A suggestion might be to give students the questions during the final examination and ask them to complete and return the form after they have received their final grade. Returns and their representativeness are problematical.

Source: William W. Ronan, *Evaluating College Classroom Teaching Effectiveness* (PREP Report No. 34), (Washington, DC: U.S. Government Printing Office, 1972), pp. 23-25.

7

A President's Perspective: A Rationale and Strategy for Building a Performance Appraisal Program

Richard J. Federinko

During the past ten years, community college administrators have been forced to deal with a complex array of problems principally associated with a shifting emphasis from growth to quality. Consequently, the challenges facing college administrators today have never been greater. Faced with declining or fluctuating enrollment patterns, diminishing financial resources, increasing expenditures associated with rapidly advancing technological changes, and pressing needs to provide a significant leadership role in economic development activities, community colleges are being asked to accomplish more with less with greater efficiency and effectiveness. As a result, institutions must implement management systems and parameters which provide for greater accountability through effective planning, managing, and evaluating.[1]

Accountability is not a fad or "buzz" word that is going to fade away. Elected officials at all levels, as well as their constituents, are demanding increased focus upon what is necessary, valuable, and productive. The focus and growing pressure on public institutions for greater accountability has resulted in an ever-increasing emphasis to examine more closely the quality of institutional programs and services. However, institutions cannot be held accountable, only individuals. Thus, growing numbers of states are requiring some form of serious performance appraisal strategy for public education employees.

Since accountability is an issue that is here to stay, the time has arrived for the community college leaders of this country to take a serious approach to developing effective, periodic, systematic, and comprehensive appraisal programs. Such programs must be based on clearly articulated criteria and must be legally defensible. Further, the appraisal process should take a positive approach as a professional development aide. No one employee should be excused, and no one should be treated differently.

The major reason for performance appraisal focuses on its use as an important tool in building institutional excellence and accountability. This would seem to be reason enough. It is not; considering the ideal of self regulation. Do we want to maintain the prerogative of managing this activity or do we want someone to do it for us or to us?

As has been well stated by John Kingdon, "If you're not ready to paddle when the big wave comes along, you're not going to ride on it."[2] The objective of this chapter is to present a strategy for developing and implementing a performance appraisal program in a postsecondary institution. The following material draws heavily on the experience of Southern Union State Junior College to demonstrate how a rather significant endeavor of this nature can be accomplished.

Assumptions About People

Writing in the late 1950s, Douglas M. McGregor was one of the first writers to suggest that administrators who hold different assumptions about people in their organizations will behave differently toward them as well. This, of course, is the basis for McGregor's famous set of assumptions known as Theory X and Theory Y.[3]

Recall that if administrators feel subordinates are lazy, indifferent, and uncooperative, they will treat them that way. Conversely, if it is assumed that their subordinates are hard-working, open-minded, and interested in achieving organizational objectives, they will treat them quite differently. The irony is that consistent with reinforcement theory, people will tend to live up to expectations; in other words, treat people as losers and they will begin to act like losers. McGregor called this result a self-fulfilling prophecy.

While McGregor's work is almost 30 years old and has received some criticism, the real value is that an administrator influences a situation by his/her assumptions about people. A number of other researchers have demonstrated the effect that expectations and environmental pressures have on human behavior. In particular, researchers such as John Roueche and George Baker recommend shifts from rigid, traditional forms of government to models of governance which are more humanistic and create a work environment that is caring and nurturing.[4] Leadership assumptions and governance styles clearly impact upon employee performance.

In regard to performance appraisal, the administration would do well to provide a positive governance style which assumes that people want to do a good job and will not only accept performance appraisal, but will demonstrate a high degree of cooperation in carrying out a program to which they become committed. Therefore, adopt the Theory Y assumptions. There is nothing to lose and a great deal to be gained.

Coping With the Literature

As would be the base with any major endeavor, it is a good idea to review the published research on performance appraisal. Several words of caution are in order. First, the amount of literature on the subject is overwhelming. It is simply impossible to read and understand all the valuable articles, books, and monographs that have been published in the past 5 to 10 years alone. If the sheer volume is not problem enough, many of the findings are discouraging. In fact, many studies conclude that little progress has been made in developing an efficient, cost effective, and psychometrically sound technique of performance appraisal.[5]

Consider, however, a different perspective. There are few, if any, other administrative functions and processes in which there are proven methods. In fact, the state-of-the-art in management is just as much a "jungle" as when Harold Koontz wrote his classic article.[6] But that doesn't seem to stop us in other activities. For example, the personnel selection process has the most far reaching consequences of any activity in administration. No researcher has ever devised a "perfect" selection test for any job; the best predictors of job success are only slightly better than chance. Yet we hire people like we know what we are doing. In fact, we also pay, promote, and develop people based on imperfect theories.

This is not to disparage the literature. Review it but do not be intimidated by it. There are a number of behavioral and outcome concepts and techniques that have been shown to work reasonably well. In fact, such authorities as Redfern and Scriven have developed models for public school systems and much of their work is useful in post-secondary education.[7] There are other methods such as trait rating scales, unstructured and impressionistic systems, and other non-job-related approaches which work poorly, if at all. An examination of the different approaches should lead to a program that best fits the needs of the institution.

Overcoming Fears and Apprehension

All members of the institutional community need to be sold on the performance appraisal program. Participatory management is itself a long-term performance strategy; on the other hand, a "top down" view invites failure.

One essential feature is an administrative mechanism for higher levels of management to review performance ratings, reinforced by an appeals procedure. A committee or group should be established to adjudicate disputed ratings and the group should include peers. The appeals procedure is particularly important in cases of demotion, suspension, or discharge for poor performance. It is also necessary to hold free and open discussions with all segments of an institution. It is at forums such as these that fears can be allayed and apprehensions addressed. These come in the form of the inevitable "what if?" questions and almost always involve a worst case scenario. It is usually possible to turn these negatives around. For example, an instructor might ask, "What if my department chair gives me a low rating because he dislikes me?" It can be pointed out that the rating criteria represent items that can be observed or measured; and that the department chair will be rated on how well he/she observes and measures performance. In fact, it can be clearly shown that a good performance appraisal system makes it difficult to award ratings on likes and dislikes; it is in the absence of such a system that biased ratings are likely to occur.

Superiors are often concerned that subordinates will resent being given low ratings on those aspects of the job where performance is deficient or will be uncooperative and resist performance appraisal altogether. The answer is that some people are difficult, but they are probably that way long before performance appraisal was instituted. The performance appraisal process itself provides a means to address certain aspects of these problems. Moreover, most administrators will agree that dealing with difficult people is a fact of organizational life and comes with the job. It is also useful to ask superiors to review their own assumptions about people to avoid McGregor's self-fulfilling prophecy.

Finally, it will probably be necessary to address the concerns of professional associations and possibly unions. These organizations may view with suspicion an administrative activity which might be used to threaten job security or undermine well established seniority systems. While it may not be possible to gain their wholehearted endorsement of performance appraisal, it is best not to adopt a confrontational approach. At a minimum, be willing to "meet and confer" and establish as much common ground as possible. Keep in mind these organizations also have a stake in the accountability issue and face the same pressures felt by institutional administrators.

For everyone concerned, the best approach is to promote a positive climate of mutual trust. Most superiors want to be fair, and most subordinates will accept honest ratings. The key is a well respected concept of common law known as "good faith and fair dealing."

Using Consultants

Most two-year colleges will require some outside assistance to develop an effective and legally defensible performance appraisal program. There are a number of possible sources. These might include the state department or division of postsecondary education, extension units and/or faculty members of major universities, and private consultants. At Southern Union we contracted with a nearby university which assembled a team of faculty members and graduate students representing several disciplinary areas: counseling, industrial psychology, foundations of education, educational administration, and management.

In assembling resources to undertake such a project, the following steps should prove useful:

- Identify potential internal resources from the faculty and administration.

- Appoint a project coordinator.

- Conduct a needs assessment and determine the expertise required.

- In selecting consultants, identify if possible persons with both professional expertise and successful experience in an educational setting.

Even if all or most of the technical assistance is obtained from consultants, it is neither necessary nor desirable to relinquish control of the project. A "lock and key" job by "outside experts" will have little credibility with the administration and support staff and practically none with the faculty. It is the institution, not the consultants, who have to live with the results.

Before the start of the project, hold a round table discussion with the consultants. Discuss with them the purposes you intend to accomplish; the funds available; services the institution will provide; documentation to be provided; pilot testing; suggested methods and techniques for various job families, follow-up activities such as rater training, validity studies, legal defense (expert witness) evaluation, and similar issues. Moreover, recognize that an undertaking of this magnitude will not be completed within a short time-frame. Participatory type involvement requires time and an abundance of patience.

Who is Covered

The major goal in performance appraisal should be to access individual work related contributions within the total institution--not just the faculty, nor the administration, nor the support staff. A performance appraisal program should be for everyone, beginning with the president. There should be, of course, different procedures for different job families. The performance of a dean is measured in terms of outcomes such as goals achieved and expectations met while the performance a library technician is expressed in terms of appropriate job-related behaviors. But in the final analysis, each person's performance is rated against a standard.

While there is disagreement in the literature on rating formats and rating scales, it is necessary to develop appropriate instrumentation. At Southern Union there are three subsystems; however, they each follow the same rules of combination and produce a rating on a 5-point scale. Thus, a department chair, instructor, and custodian who receive an overall rating of "3.5" are performing at the same level, albeit in vastly different roles.

Legality

When used as input to decisions such as retention, promotion, and merit increases, performance appraisal results have important legal implications. Even when used only for developmental purposes, it might be difficult to establish the fact that ratings have no bearing on administrative decisions. People are protected by federal laws and court decisions from discrimination based on race, color, sex, religion, national origin, age, physical handicap, and Veteran status. Moreover, the common law doctrine of employment-at-will has been significantly eroded in state courts. Therefore, it is extremely important that the performance appraisal system be validated in accordance with appropriate regulations.[8]

While no performance appraisal system can be made grievance proof or immune to litigation, a properly designed validity study is an essential document when and if performance ratings are called into question by a regulatory agency or a court. The study should address such critical issues as job analysis, criterion development, instrumentation, procedures, and purposes. Without evidence of validity, even systems designed by "experts" are likely to be rejected by the courts.

Management Support

When beginning the implementation phase of a performance appraisal program, often the president or another administrator makes appropriate comments at a convocation or issues a letter pledging his/her support. All this is fine if preceded by intimate involvement in the developmental phase and followed by a demonstrated personal commitment. If performance appraisal is to be taken seriously, managers and supervisors at all levels of the institution must be conscientiously involved. In fact, how well they accomplish this task should be reflected in their performance ratings.

Shakedown Administration

No matter how competent and professional the team that developed the program, or how high the level of management support, or how deeply involved were the faculty and staff from its inception, there will be problems in implementation. Behavioral anchors which were clear and concise when written and reviewed by 15 people in three levels of the organization will suddenly become vague and ambiguous. Rater errors and tendencies which were fully covered during rater training sessions will proliferate and several new ones will emerge. Carefully designed weighting systems and rules of combination will come apart when the same people who signed off on the job analysis data point out that the criteria do not match their work assignments. When the dust settles, it will be discovered that the problems are not that serious and can be corrected without fundamental changes. The time to make these refinements, however, is during a shakedown administration or "dry run." It is not when the ratings are to be used for administrative decisions.

Concluding Remarks

Designing, developing, and implementing an effective performance appraisal system is not an easy task. In fact, the Southern Union process at times could have been described as difficult, confusing, controversial, and time-consuming. But, "difficulty and confusion" were addressed early from the process by retaining individuals with professional expertise in implementing a sophisticated, comprehensive appraisal system. "Controversy" was mitigated through total institutional commitment, involvement, negotiation, and communication. As far as the "time-consuming" aspect of the process, this is one factor which simply cannot nor ever will be eliminated. In fact, maintenance of the appraisal process at Southern Union continues to be time-consuming. Effective performance appraisal systems require continuous refinement and modification because position descriptions will be rearranged, errors will be found, new positions will evolve, and humans will change for the sake of change. Change, therefore, is a necessary ingredient in the evolution of an effective system of appraisal.

At Southern Union, the "high road" to developing and implementing a performance appraisal system was taken. A genuinely open and positive environment was created, disagreement was expected, negotiation was required, and individual participation by everyone was necessary. Through total institutional commitment, a very positive outcome was achieved. But more important, Southern Union wisely invested in the positive development of its greatest resource: its individual employees. Its employees are consequently highly motivated, achievement-oriented, and committed to accountability.

Endnotes

1.   Gerald L. McManis and L. James Harvey, *Planning, Management and Evaluation Systems in Higher Education*, (Littleton: Ireland, 1978), p. 1.

2.   John W. Kingdon, *Agendas Alternative and Public Policies*, (Boston, Little, Brown, 1984), p. 173.

3.   Douglas McGregor, *The Human Side of Enterprise*, (New York: McGraw-Hill, 1960).

4.   John E. Roueche and George A. Baker, III, *Beacons for Change: An Innovative Outcome Model for Community Colleges*, (Iowa: American College Testing, 1983), pp. 1-3.

5.   For an excellent discussion of these issues, see Arthur M. Cohen and Florence B. Brawer, *Confronting Identity: The Community College Instructor*, (Englewood Cliffs, NJ: Prentice-Hall, 1972).

6.   Harold Koontz, "The Management Theory Jungle," *Journal of the Academy of Management* 4 (December 1961), pp. 174-188.

7.   See, for example, George B. Redfern, *Evaluating Teachers and Administrators: A Performance Objectives Approach*, (Boulder, CO: Westview, 1982) and Michael Scriven "Summative Teacher Education," in *Handbook of Teacher Education*, ed. Jason Millman (Beverly Hills, CA: Sage, 1981).

8.   An excellent analysis of the various legal constraints that impact on the personnel function can be found in James Ledvinka, *Federal Regulation of Personnel and Human Resource Management*, (Boston: Kent, 1982), pp. 1-114 and particularly pp. 19-51 and pp. 91-101.

8

Characteristics of Effective and Legally Defensible Performance Appraisal Systems for Postsecondary Education

Bettye B. Burkhalter and James A. Buford, Jr.

Performance appraisal continues to be one of the most important responsibilities of administrators in postsecondary institutions. It increasingly is becoming a legal prob lem; the growth of federal laws and regulations has created specific rights for faculty and staff in their relationship with their employers. Characteristics of a performance appraisal system that accurately measures job contributions and is completely defensible in today's legal environment continue to be a matter of debate. Such a system may not exist. However, incorporation of the following will minimize many of the most common legal problems and lead to a more effective system.

1. *Needs Assessment and Planning.* An institution that is considering perfor-mance appraisal should decide in advance what the program is intended to accomplish. Uses of performance ratings might include input to placement, promotion, compensa-tion, development, and termination decisions. Only after the purpose is clearly estab-lished and the specific requirements are decided upon is the organization in a position to develop a performance appraisal program.

2. *Participation.* Research clearly has shown that work is a motivator and that most people want to do a good job.[1] A well respected philosophy is that the authority in an organization is delegated upward. Thus, it makes intuitive sense that people at every level need to participate in the development of a performance appraisal program. If they do not, it will be very difficult to gain their understanding and support during implementation.

3. *Job Analysis.* The cornerstone of the development of a performance appraisal system is job analysis.[2,3] When an employment practice is to be defended on the basis of content validity, the job analysis establishes the rational link between factors used in appraisal and the critical work behaviors of the job.[4] Two comprehen-sive reviews of characteristics of performance appraisal systems related to court decisions found that where job analysis was performed, courts ruled in favor of the defendants in approximately 82 percent of the cases. Without job analysis, defendants

lost every case.[5] Job analysis should be conducted when duties are reasonably stable so that conditions will be comparable to those which will exist when the performance appraisal instrument is used.

4. *Performance Criteria.* While traits such as initiative, enthusiasm, attitude, and loyalty are important to job performance, most often they are not suitable as performance criteria.[6,7] It is better to develop criteria which describe observable job behaviors or outcomes. Even when the possession of a trait can be shown as critical for effective job performance, it is usually possible to design an observable measurement based on how job duties actually are performed.

5. *Appraisal Instruments.* The various instruments should facilitate the administration of performance appraisal under standardized and controlled conditions.[8] Instruments should be designed carefully to accommodate both the criteria and method. If several criteria or scales are to be combined, the instrument should produce a composite rating based on the rules of combination.[9] Appropriate identification, comments, and signatory sections should be included.

6. *Reliability and Validity.* To achieve the organization's purpose of accurately measuring performance and to satisfy legal requirements, the appraisal system must be valid; it must measure what it purports to measure. First, however, the system must be reliable. The ratings must yield stable and consistent results from one period to the next and across all items.[10] Reliability and validity studies should be conducted to meet technical standards of the "Uniform Guidelines on Employee Selection Procedures" and documented in a written report.[11]

7. *Testing the System.* Prior to implementation of performance appraisal, a review should be conducted to ensure that the process selected supports overall objectives and will provide the needed information flow to such decision areas as compensation, placement, and professional development. In many cases it may be necessary to conduct a pilot or "shakedown" test of the system to identify and address problem areas and work out procedural matters.[12]

8. *Communication of Policy and Purpose.* The purpose and uses of performance appraisal should be stated clearly in the organizational policy as well as in the employee or faculty handbook. Procedures should be developed to cover which systems will be used for which jobs or job families, how often appraisals are to be conducted, documentation required, recourse, and similar matters. Fully informing all individuals of policies will minimize uncertainty and resistance and will increase the probability of positive results.[13]

9. *Rater Training.* In many organizations, the task of observing and measuring job performance is poorly carried out. Research has indicated that rater training is more important than design considerations in improving accuracy of performance appraisal. Training programs should focus on improving rater skills in observing, recording, and appraising behavior with less emphasis given to such issues as rating distributions and

statistical measures.[14] Extremely good results have been obtained with training programs designed to build observational skills and reduce such common problems as halo effect, first impressions, patterns of leniency and strictness, recency, and similar errors.[15] Raters must fully understand the critical importance of the interpersonal aspects of performance appraisal. They must develop skills in feedback, praise, constructive criticism, and listening. Raters also must be sensitive to the situations and conditions faced by individuals. Finally, raters must develop skills for identifying, describing, and negotiating performance expectations.

10. *Administration.* The most basic requirement is that the performance appraisal process should support the system's goals; conflicting multiple uses should be avoided. The system could be cost effective. Expenses should be balanced against the post appraisal impact on motivation and productivity.[16] Performance appraisal administration must ensure that the people who are being rated understand the mechanics, including such issues as performance expectations, how ratings on various criteria will be weighted, and who will actually conduct the appraisal. Finally, it is very important that performance appraisal be conducted by raters who have directed and continually observed job performance.[17]

11. *Privacy and Due Process.* The Federal Privacy Act of 1973 created the Privacy Protection Study Committee (PPSC), which issued a series of recommendations in 1977. Among these was the suggestion that employees should have access to all records relating to their qualifications for employment, promotion, and pay increases and to records relating to discipline and discharge. Many professional groups have recommended voluntary compliance with these recommendations. Moreover, individual access to records builds confidence in the system's basic fairness, provides an additional means of communicating results, and protects the individual's rights.[18] Adverse performance ratings can lead to denial of merit pay and promotions in some cases, dismissal. Due process refers to a systematic, orderly procedure where an individual has the opportunity to object and be heard.[19] Employee rights in this area are still evolving; however, courts increasingly are requiring employers to justify their actions.[20] Legal questions aside, organizations due process is a good management practice. A formal appeal process should be established to provide an impartial review of ratings that are disputed.

12. *Audits.* Performance ratings should be analyzed periodically for evidence of discrepancies and adverse impact. Statistical tests do not prove that raters are making errors or showing bias. However, properly designed analyses can highlight certain patterns that might not be found merely by reviewing a list of ratings. When such patterns appear, management should determine the cause and, if necessary, correct the problem--particularly when members of protected groups such as blacks and females receive significantly lower ratings.

In the final analysis, the effectiveness and legal defensibility of a performance appraisal system will depend on its legitimacy as a tool for making employment decisions. The success of any system depends on its effective administration by all levels of management. A common failure of performance appraisal systems is the assumption that forms, handbooks, and policy statements are just another set of procedures. No appraisal program, regardless of how well it is developed, will be effective or legally defensible unless administrators have a high level of commitment and make a continuous effort to carry out the complete process. A poor system can be made to work when the administrators make the effort to compensate for inadequacies in design. On the other hand, if a state-of-the-art system is poorly administered, it will surely fail.

Endnotes

1. Frederick Herzberg, Bernard Mausner, and Barbara B. Snyderman, *The Motivation of Work*, (New York: Wiley, 1959).

2. Gary P. Latham and Kenneth N. Wexley, *Increasing Productivity Through Performance Appraisal*, (Reading, MA: Addison-Wesley, 1981), p. 73.

3. *Kirkland v. New York State Department of Corrections*, 374F. Supp. 1361 (S.D.N.Y.), 1974.

4. Richard E. Biddle, *Guidelines Oriented Job Analysis*, Section 5 (Sacramento: Biddle and Associates, 1976), p. 1.

5. Hubert S. Feild and William H. Holley, "The Relationship of Performance Appraisal System Characteristics to Verdicts in Selected Employment Discrimination Cases," *Academy of Management Journal* 25 (June 1982) pp. 392-406. A follow-up study was conducted for the period 1980-1983 and produced similar results. See Hubert S. Feild and D. T. Thompson, "Study of Court Decisions in Cases Involving Performance Appraisal," *Bureau of National Affairs, Daily Labor Report*, No. 248 December 26, 1984, pp. E1-E5.

6. Ronald G. Wells, "Guidelines for Effective and Defensible Performance Appraisal Systems," *Personnel Journal* 61 (October 1982), p. 777.

7. *Wade v. Mississippi Cooperative Extension Service*, 372F. Supp. 126, 7 EPD 9186 (1974).

8. *Brito v. Zia Company*, 478F. 2D. 1200 (1973).

9. Latham and Wexley, *op. cit.*, p. 73.

10. Fred N. Kellinger, *Foundations of Behavioral Research* 2nd ed. (New York Holt, Rinehart & Winston, 1964); Chapters 26 and 27 provide an in-depth discussion of reliability and validity.

11. Equal Employment Opportunity Commission, Civil Service Commission Department of Labor and Department of Justice, "Uniform Guidelines on Employee Selection Procedures," *Federal Register* 43 (August 25, 1978), pp. 38290-38315.

12. Latham and Wexley, *op. cit.*, p. 73.

13. Wells, *op. cit.*, p. 777.

14. Gary P. Latham, Kenneth N. Wexley, and Elliot D. Pursell, "Training Managers to Minimize Rating Errors in the Observation of Behavior," *Journal of Applied Psychology* 60 (October 1975), pp. 550-555.

15. Charles H. Fay and Gary P. Latham, "Effects of Training and Ratings Scales on Rating Errors," *Personnel Psychology* 35 (Spring 1982), pp. 105-116.

16. Seleg M. Danzig. "What We Need to Know About Performance Appraisals," *Management Review* 69 (February 1980), p. 21.

17. Biddle, *op. cit.*, pp. 11-12.

18. Wells, *op. cit.*, p. 781.

19. William H. Holley and Kenneth M. Jennings, *Personnel Management* 2nd ed. (Chicago: Dryden, 1983), p. 612.

20. See, for example, *Board of Regents of State Colleges et al. v. Roth*, 408 U.S. 564 (1972). Over the past 15 years, *Roth* has been followed by a long series of decisions in federal and state courts usually taking the side of the employee. Legal bases to sue include breach of contract, violation of public policy, "bad faith," and discrimination. For a detailed review see Daniel M. Mackey, *Employment at Will and Employer Liability*, (New York: American Managment Association, 1986).

Appendices

Appendix A: Performance Appraisal Forms*

Appendix A contains case examples of performance appraisal forms designed for a variety of jobs within The Alabama College System. The types of forms vary depending on the different job category--support, administrative, or faculty. However, the basis for all appraisal instruments in detailed job analysis which categorizes job duties into major responsibility areas, or job domains. These domains are weighted based on frequency and importance of duties. On each performance appraisal form appropriate job domains are listed along with their assigned weights. A five-point rating scale is employed throughout, with space designated for explanatory comments. At this point, the appraisal approach varies, depending on the type of job. Explanations of each exhibit will follow.

---

*Exhibits 1-4 in this appendix were developed by Anne Smyth Stewart, M.Ed., Counselor, Student Development Services, Auburn University, AL 36849. Exhibit 5 in this appendix was developed by Deborah J. Miller-Wood, M.A., Graduate Research Associate, Department of Educational Foundations, Leadership, and Technology, Auburn University, AL 36849.

Exhibit 1

The job of Library Technician at Southern Union State Junior College falls into the support category. Jobs in this group are appraised using the weighted responsibility areas as performance criteria. These are identified in Part II of the *Performance Appraisal Form* and are defined using qualifying words that state "how" a set of duties is performed. The performance discussion and summary in Part III deals with factors that impact on the overall performance and should be self explanatory.

PERFORMANCE APPRAISAL FORM

Southern Union State Junior College

PART I   IDENTIFICATION

Name _____

Position __Library Technician_____

Rating Period From _____ To _____

Rater Name _____

Rater Title _____

Department _____

Date Employed _____

Rating Scale Key

1 Fails to Meet Job Requirements
2 Essentially Meets Job Requirements
3 Fully Meets Job Requirements
4 Meets Job Requirements with Distinction
5 Exceeds Job Requirements

PART II   RATING SCALES FOR MAJOR RESPONSIBILITIES

A. **Physical Processing** PCT. 35 %	RATING: 1 ☐ 2 ☐ 3 ☐ 4 ☐ 5 ☐
Creating and maintaining records, and correctly performing related tasks needed to facilitate locating and obtaining library materials.	COMMENTS
B. **Circulation** PCT. 20 %	RATING: 1 ☐ 2 ☐ 3 ☐ 4 ☐ 5 ☐
Carrying out prescribed procedures, and accurately maintaining records regarding the borrowing of books and other materials by library users.	COMMENTS
C. **Acquisition** PCT. 15 %	RATING: 1 ☐ 2 ☐ 3 ☐ 4 ☐ 5 ☐
Ordering and receiving books, periodicals, and other materials; and accurately maintaining records.	COMMENTS
D. **Reference** PCT. 10 %	RATING: 1 ☐ 2 ☐ 3 ☐ 4 ☐ 5 ☐
Assisting library users by providing information services, answering questions, assisting in locating library materials, and integrating information into cataloging system.	COMMENTS
E. **Cataloging and Classification** PCT. 10 %	RATING: 1 ☐ 2 ☐ 3 ☐ 4 ☐ 5 ☐
Accurately compiling information and properly entering classifications of library materials, and integrating information into cataloging system.	COMMENTS
F. **General and Administrative** PCT. 10 %	RATING: 1 ☐ 2 ☐ 3 ☐ 4 ☐ 5 ☐
Carrying out administrative support services and activities in accordance with institution policies and procedures.	COMMENTS
G. PCT. %	RATING: 1 ☐ 2 ☐ 3 ☐ 4 ☐ 5 ☐
	COMMENTS

PART III   PERFORMANCE DISCUSSION AND SUMMARY

Does the employee report for and remain at work as required?   ☐ yes   ☐ no   If no, please explain.

Does the employee follow instructions and observe work rules?   ☐ yes   ☐ no   If no, please explain.

Does the employee get along and cooperate with co-workers on the job?   ☐ yes   ☐ no   If no, please explain.

Does the employee have the knowledges, skills, abilities, and other qualifications needed for successful job performance?   ☐ yes   ☐ no   If no, please explain.

Describe any specific actions employee needs to take to improve job performance.

Summarize this employee's overall job performance as determined in your joint discussion.

PART IV   SIGNATURES

This report is based on my observation and knowledge of both the employee and the job.

My signature indicates that I have reviewed this appraisal. It does not mean that I agree with the results.

_____
Supervisor   Date

_____
Reviewer   Date

_____
Employee   Date

Exhibit 2

The position of Director, Instructional and Student Development, is a state level administrative position. The *sample Performance Appraisal Form* shown is similar to that used in Exhibit 1, with key expectations included as an added dimension. Weighted job domains are entered on the form and defined in performance-related terms. Key expectations for the rating period will have been entered from the previous review session when these were developed. Each of these areas is then rated against the five-point scale. Part III addresses factors which impact on the performance of the job but do not fall under specific duty statements. These are not rated on a scale; rather are discussed in narrative form. The remaining sections of this form are self-explanatory.

PERFORMANCE APPRAISAL FORM

Name _____ Identification Number _____

Title _____ Director _____ Division Instructional and Student Development

Date Employed _____ Date Assigned Present Job _____

Rater Name _____ Title _____

Appraisal Period: From _____ To _____

This Appraisal Is: _____ Annual _____ Other

INSTRUCTIONS

PART I. PERFORMANCE RESPONSIBILITY RATINGS

The position responsibilities are taken from the job description. The rater appraises results achieved against responsibilities/expectations by checking one of the five following degrees:

5 - EXCEPTIONAL. Performance which clearly exceeds work requirements and indicates an exceptional desire and ability to do more than is reasonably expected in terms of professional quality, work output, or both.

4 - VERY GOOD. Performance which meets work requirements with distinction and indicates a desire and ability to do a highly professional job.

3 - ACCEPTABLE. Performance which fully meets work requirements and indicates a desire and ability to do a thorough and competent job.

2 - MARGINAL. Performance which essentially meets work requirements and indicates a desire and ability to be at least adequate.

1 - UNACCEPTABLE. Performance which clearly fails to meet work requirements and indicates either a lack of ability or unwillingness to do what is reasonably expected.

Read the definitions of each performance responsibility, including the expectations or objectives which have been established; then appraise the person by one responsibility at a time. Omit appraisal on any responsibility for which you believe your observation has been insufficient or which did not apply to the person. Disregard your general impression of the person and concentrate on the performance responsibility definitions established. Rate the person on his/her typical performance on that responsibility during the entire rating period.

Raters can appraise performance on those criteria which the rater has *regularly* and *directly* observed *or* where there is objective evidence. Ratings must be based on *facts.* Do not be influenced by previous ratings. While it is true that several responsibilities are related, when you rate a person on one responsibility, you must disregard the ratings you have given him/her on other responsibilities. For any factor which your appraisal is either UNACCEPTABLE or EXCEPTIONAL, justify with appropriate comments. In addition, comments should be made for *any* rating if they will clarify your rating.

PART II. PERFORMANCE FACTORS

Comment on each of the factors which influenced performance in assigned responsibilities. Use specific examples and, as appropriate, emphasize both strengths and areas needing improvement. Comments should not focus on personality traits or personal habits but rather on how they translate into observed behaviors in getting the job done. If a factor was not applicable during the rating period, leave it blank. The performance factors, while not directly rated, are important in understanding how results were achieved and in identifying ways to improve performance in succeeding periods.

PART III. SUMMARY PERFORMANCE STATEMENT

The Summary Performance Statement is a key part of the performance appraisal. It should summarize the overall results, the manner in which results were achieved, any special conditions which existed, and the trend of performance.

PART IV. STAFF MEMBER'S COMMENTS

In this section, the staff member should be encouraged to make specific comments on any aspect of his/her performance appraisal.

PART V. SIGNATURES

Following the performance appraisal discussion, the rater and staff member will sign the appraisal form. It will then be forwarded through channels to the Chancellor for review and signatures.

PART I. PERFORMANCE RESPONSIBILITY RATINGS

Enter performance responsibility areas from job description and include relative importance. Enter standards, objectives, or other expectations for the rating period. Make comments on observed job behaviors and results achieved. Rate performance based on definitions provided.

A. Administration (25%). Effectively analyzing the situation for the Division, setting goals, and developing policies, operating plans, and assignments; submitting accurate, timely reports.	
KEY EXPECTATIONS FOR RATING PERIOD:	COMMENTS: 1 2 3 4 5 RATING ☐ ☐ ☐ ☐ ☐

B. Instructional Programs (20%). Providing instructional leadership for the system through coordination of Division staff and task forces in curriculum development and design, standardization of courses, competency-based instructional approaches and program evaluation.	
KEY EXPECTATIONS FOR RATING PERIOD:	COMMENTS: 1 2 3 4 5 RATING ☐ ☐ ☐ ☐ ☐

C. Supervisory Management (20%). Selecting, training, and appraising staff, directing the activities of subordinates toward the accomplishment of objectives; and promoting efficiency.	
KEY EXPECTATIONS FOR RATING PERIOD:	COMMENTS: 1 2 3 4 5 RATING ☐ ☐ ☐ ☐ ☐

D. Liaison and Special Services (15%) Effectively representing the Chancellor and the department in official matters; performing other related services as assigned.	
KEY EXPECTATIONS FOR RATING PERIOD:	COMMENTS: 1 2 3 4 5 RATING ☐ ☐ ☐ ☐ ☐

E. Faculty/Staff Policies and Development (10%). Developing and maintaining policies for faculty/staff at all institutions; providing opportunities and a structure through which instructors can increase or improve credentials, skills and abilities.	
KEY EXPECTATIONS FOR RATING PERIOD:	COMMENTS: 1 2 3 4 5 RATING ☐ ☐ ☐ ☐ ☐

F. Student Services (10%). Providing leadership for student services through the professional staff of the Division and through student services departments at each institution.	
KEY EXPECTATIONS FOR RATING PERIOD:	COMMENTS: 1 2 3 4 5 RATING ☐ ☐ ☐ ☐ ☐

KEY EXPECTATIONS FOR RATING PERIOD:	COMMENTS:
	RATING 1 □ 2 □ 3 □ 4 □ 5 □

KEY EXPECTATIONS FOR RATING PERIOD:	COMMENTS:
	RATING 1 □ 2 □ 3 □ 4 □ 5 □

PART II. PERFORMANCE FACTORS

Comment on each of the factors which influenced performance of assigned responsibilities and how they translated into observed behaviors.

FACTOR	COMMENTS
Self Development and Appraisal - How effectively this person analyzes own performance, strengths, and weaknesses; accepts constructive criticism; participates in relevant education experiences; reads job-related literature; keeps up-to-date on new trends and developments; and improves capabilities to meet changing job requirements.	
Administrative Skills - How effectively this person recognizes priorities, formulates schedules, establishes work objectives, understands or defines responsibilties, projects work needs, organizes the work to be performed, and in general avoids "crisis" types of activities.	
Interpersonal Relations - How effectively this person interacts with superiors, subordinates, peers, and external contacts in both favorable and unfavorable or conflict situations.	
Oral Communications - How effectively this person verbally communicates information including using appropriate language, listening, overcoming barriers, and obtaining feedback in situations involving either information transfer or persuasion.	
Written Communications - How effectively this person produces written material which is clear, concise, expressed in a logical and direct manner, correct in grammar and spelling, and presented in the appropriate format and style.	

PART III. SUMMARY PERFORMANCE STATEMENT

Summarize overall results, manner in which results were achieved, special conditions under which performance occurred, developmental needs, and trend of performance.

PART IV. STAFF MEMBER'S COMMENTS

Please use the space below to comment on any aspect of your performance appraisal.

PART V. SIGNATURES

Rater:

_____   _____   _____
Signature   Title   Date

Staff Member:

I have reviewed and discussed this performance appraisal with my superior. I am aware that I have the opportunity to comment on this performance appraisal in writing and that my comments will become part of the record of this performance appraisal.

_____   _____   _____
Signature   Title   Date

Reviewers:

_____   _____   _____
Signature   Title   Date

_____   _____   _____
Signature   Title   Date

Exhibit 3

There are two forms used for the administrative position, Dean of Instruction. In the document entitled *Performance Standards*, each domain is broken down into sub-criteria for which performance standards are developed. These are written at the "meets standards" level as an anchor for the performance rating. The degree to which standards are met, exceeded, or not met will determine the rating assigned on the document entitled *Performance Appraisal Form*. For administrative positions at this level, setting annual objectives and assessing results are key parts of performance appraisal. Parts III and IV allow for future planning and for assessment of the previous year's objectives. The appraisal summary in Part V encourages a developmental, positive approach in discussing employee strengths and possible areas for improvement.

PERFORMANCE STANDARDS

Southern Union State Junior College

Job Title: Dean of Instruction

Department: Administration

Job Domain	Performance meets standards when:
A. Planning (20%)	1. *Long-Range Plans.* Analysis is made of situation and needs, measurable objectives are established, and appropriate plans are developed. 2. *Policies and Procedures.* Written policies, directives, handbooks, and procedures are developed and communicated in all academic and areas. 3. *Academic Calendar and Schedules.* All day and night programs, including off-campus centers, are scheduled in a cost-effective manner, with consideration for space utilization of students and qualifications and preferences of faculty members. 4. *Budget.* Development of academic budget is accomplished based on appropriate guidelines and submitted on or before deadline; adequate budgetary control procedures are established. 5. *Accreditation.* Action plans are developed to meet or maintain accreditation standards of the Southern Association of Colleges and Schools (SACS) and other accrediting agencies.
B. Organizing (10%)	1. *Organizational Structure.* Academic organizational structure is developed and implemented. Organization facilitates accomplishment of objectives. 2. *Committees.* Appropriate standing and *ad hoc* committees are established and charged. Committees carry out prescribed functions and make scheduled reports.
C. Staffing (10%)	1. *Planning and Analysis.* Adequate human resource planning for academic program is accomplished; all jobs are periodically analyzed, and comprehensive job descriptions are maintained. 2. *Personnel Functions.* Recruiting, selection, development, appraisal, and compensation functions for academic, administrative, and support positions are carried out in accordance with prescribed procedures. 3. *Legal Requirements.* All personnel procedures are validated in accordance with current EEO laws and guidelines.
D. Leading and Directing (25%)	1. *Overall Leadership.* Policies, procedures, rules, directives, and instructions are clearly communicated to subordinates at all levels; administrators, chairpersons, and supervisors at all levels use interpersonal influence, lead by example, and promote teamwork; a climate is established where academic administrative staff and faculty are motivated in work toward objectives; developing problems are identified and expeditiously resolved at lowest possible level in organizational structure; and progressive discipline is used, employee rights to due process are protected, and procedures are followed in all cases.

page 1 of 2

E. Controlling and Reporting (20%)	1. *Concurrent Control.* Key indicators of performance are established and activities are monitored in all academic areas; corrections are made where necessary. 2. *Feedback Control.* Accomplishments are compared against plans and standards at end of performance/budget cycle. Analysis is made of any failure to accomplish planned results and appropriate action is taken. 3. *Reports.* All regular and special reports are accurately prepared and submitted on time. Information from reports is analyzed and used in planning process.
F. External Affairs (10%)	1. *Public Relations.* Good public relations are maintained with community, legislative delegations, and other educational institutions to encourage maximum contribution by external groups to college objectives. 2. *Representation.* A positive image of the college is projected.
G. Professional Development (5%)	1. *Credentials.* Incumbent holds appropriate terminal degree. 2. *Self-Development.* Adequate current knowledge of professional matters is maintained through attendance of meetings of professional associations, journals, workshop attendance, and personal study.

PERFORMANCE APPRAISAL FORM

Southern Union State Junior College

PART I   IDENTIFICATION

Name _____

Position ___Dean of Instruction___

Rating Period From _____ To _____

Rater Name _____

Rater Title _____

Department _____

Date Employed _____

Rating Scale Key

1	Fails to Meet Standards
2	Essentially Meets Standards
3	Fully Meets Standards
4	Meets Standards with Distinction
5	Exceeds Standards

PART II   RATING SCALES

Performance Standards For:	Rating (1 2 3 4 5)	Comments
A. **Planning** — Pct. _20_%		
1. Long-Range Plans		
2. Policies and Procedures		
3. Academic Calendar and Schedules		
4. Budget		
5. Accreditation		

Performance Standards For:	Rating (1 2 3 4 5)	Comments
B. **Organizing** — Pct. _10_%		
1. Organizational Structure		
2. Committees		
3.		
4.		
5.		

Performance Standards For:	Rating (1 2 3 4 5)	Comments
C. **Staffing** — Pct. _10_%		
1. Planning and Analysis		
2. Personnel Functions		
3. Legal Requirements		
4.		
5.		

Performance Standards For:	Rating (1 2 3 4 5)	Comments
D. **Leading and Directing** — Pct. _25_%		
1. Overall Leadership		
2. Academic Program		
3.		
4.		
5.		

Performance Standards For:	Rating	Comments
E. **Controlling and Reporting** Pct. **15** %	1 2 3 4 5	
1. Concurrent Control	☐ ☐ ☐ ☐ ☐	
2. Feedback Control	☐ ☐ ☐ ☐ ☐	
3. Reports	☐ ☐ ☐ ☐ ☐	
4. _____	☐ ☐ ☐ ☐ ☐	
5. _____		

Performance Standards For:	Rating	Comments
F. **External Affairs** Pct. **10** %	1 2 3 4 5	
1. Public Relations	☐ ☐ ☐ ☐ ☐	
2. Representation	☐ ☐ ☐ ☐ ☐	
3. _____	☐ ☐ ☐ ☐ ☐	
4. _____	☐ ☐ ☐ ☐ ☐	
5. _____		

Performance Standards For:	Rating	Comments
G. **Professional Development** Pct. **5** %	1 2 3 4 5	
1. Credentials	☐ ☐ ☐ ☐ ☐	
2. Self-Development	☐ ☐ ☐ ☐ ☐	
3. _____	☐ ☐ ☐ ☐ ☐	
4. _____	☐ ☐ ☐ ☐ ☐	
5. _____		

PART III   OBJECTIVES

Key End Result	Measure

Performance Assessment

Key End Result	Measure

Performance Assessment

Key End Result	Measure
Performance Assessment	

Key End Result	Measure
Performance Assessment	

PART IV OBJECTIVES-NEXT REVIEW PERIOD

Key End Result	Measure

Key End Result	Measure

Key End Result	Measure

Key End Result	Measure

PART V   DEVELOPMENTAL APPRAISAL SUMMARY

PART VI   SIGNATURES

This report is based on
my observation and
knowledge of both the
employee and the job.

My signature indicates that
I have reviewed this appraisal.
It does not mean that I agree
with the results.

_____
Supervisor   Date

_____
Reviewer   Date

_____
Employee   Date

Exhibit 4

An expanded approach is used for the Faculty position at Southern Union State Junior College, with *Observation Scales* to be used in conjunction with the *Performance Appraisal Form*. In this case, descriptive statements are written to reflect typical behaviors at each level on the five-point scale rather than just at the number 3, "meets standards" level. Therefore, a department head completing this form on a faculty member will need to read through the scales for each criteria to locate the description best suited to the observed performance. Parts IV and V of the Performance Appraisal Form are self-explanatory.

Observation Scales for

Faculty Appraisal

and

Development

SU

Southern Union State
Junior College

A. Instructional Planning and Preparation

1. **Course Development** - Researches literature in subject area, develops and maintains course outlines, selects textbooks and other teaching aids.

   5 Exceptional   Assumes a leadership role in divisional planning meetings and other aspects of curriculum development, suggesting additional course offerings and/or modifications in current offerings. Carefully researches literature and attends workshops focusing on curriculum/course development, learning resources, and subject area matters. Serves as a resource person in subject area and offers suggestions to colleagues regarding textbooks and other learning resources.

   4 Very Good   Takes an active role in divisional planning meetings regarding curriculum or course development. Researches current literature. Shares information with colleagues. Updates course outlines and suggests ways to optimize format of course outlines.

   3 Acceptable   Shares responsibilities in divisional planning meetings regarding course development. Prepares each quarter written course outlines (syllabi) for courses taught, incorporating recent developments in subject area and current methods of instruction. Submits outline on time to Dean's office. Makes suggestions regarding textbooks and other teaching aids.

   2 Marginal   Attends divisional planning meetings and participates without taking direct responsibility. Submits course outline to Dean's office with minimal or no changes from previous years. Provides support for others' suggestions regarding textbooks and other teaching aids.

   1 Unacceptable Misses or irregularly attends divisional planning meetings. Assumes minimal or no responsibility for completing course outlines. Demonstrates limited interest in using textbooks or other resources.

2. **Instructional Planning** - Makes necessary preparations for classroom lectures, demonstrations or laboratory presentations.

   5 Exceptional   Develops, maintains, and previews additional resources, such as films or tapes for reference, timing, and quality. Utilizes a variety of teaching methods and aids. Promotes sophisticated inquiry techniques and provides problem solving experiences emphasizing key concepts. Instructional time is optimally planned for benefit of students.

4 Very Good   Develops detailed notes and guides. Presentations are well planned emphasizing key concepts. Comprehensively integrates lecture, etc. with textbook and/or other curricular materials. Instructional time and variety of material is planned for benefit of students.

3 Acceptable   Develops outlines and notes to ensure that key concepts are emphasized; that textbooks and other materials are integrated. Instructional time is wisely used. Comes to class prepared with necessary materials for classroom instruction.

2 Marginal   Reviews topic(s) to be covered. Outlines presentation or instructional activity so that instructional time is not wasted. Usually is prepared with materials necessary for class instruction.

1 Acceptable   Reflects minimal or no preparation in instructional performance. Primarily relies on textbook, outdated notes, and/or student input for class content. Arrives at class unprepared without instructional materials necessary for presentation.

3. **Clinical Preparation (Nursing)** - Provides for efficient and effective utilization of the clinical facility and staff.

5 Exceptional   Meets regularly with clinical staff or head nurse to promote a productive working relationship. Respects all levels of clinical staff. Exhibits interest and implements strategies to improve and facilitate optimal clinical experiences for students. Carefully assesses how each student's learning needs are being met by clinical experiences and arranges for modifications as necessary. Possesses thorough knowledge of facility's system, routines, procedures, and regulations.

4 Very Good   Maintains frequent contact with facility staff to ensure positive working relations. Is sensitive to the reciprocal relationship between the clinical facility and nursing program. Actively follows student progress within program. Respects and follows facility's routine, procedures, and regulations.

3 Acceptable   Maintains adequate communication with facility staff. Monitors students' progress within program. Knows and follows facility's routine, procedures, and regulations.

2 Marginal   Communications are limited with facility staff. Follows through with experiences planned by course coordinator. Seeks assistance or information from staff on occasion regarding facility's routine, procedures, and regulations.

1 Unacceptable Communications are rare with facility staff. Lacks a working knowledge about facility's routine, procedures, and regulations. Fails to seek or consider feedback from students on effectiveness of clinical experiences.

4. **Clinical Planning (Emergency Medical Technician-EMT)** - Plans experiences and assignments within clinical facility.

5 Exceptional   Acts as a facilitator to clinical staff to update plans for clinical experiences. Researches to discover innovative ways to improve and further facilitate positive clinical experiences for students. Carefully assesses how each student's needs are met through the experiences and assignments completed in the facility. Modifies experiences or assignments of students as deemed necessary.

4 Very Good   Maintains frequent contact with clinical supervisor to ensure productive working relationship. Is sensitive to the reciprocal relationship between the facility and the program. Monitors student progress throughout the quarter by encouraging feedback from supervisor on student performance and experiences. Encourages input from students on possible improvements in clinical experiences.

3 Acceptable   Holds necessary meetings with supervisor in clinical facility to plan assignments, experiences, and schedules in order to promote students' development and attainment of course objectives. Monitors student progress throughout the quarter.

2 Marginal   Maintains minimal communications with supervisors in clinical facilities. Plans for students' clinical experiences, but relies predominantly on the facility staff to dictate experiences. Usually schedules appropriate assignments. Accepts student feedback on occasion.

1 Unacceptable Communicates rarely with supervisors in clinical facilities. Fails to plan appropriate clinical experiences or relevant assignments. Discourages student feedback in clinical activities.

B. Instruction

1. **Schedule and Attendance** - Teaches classes as scheduled or requested, and encourages and records class attendance.

5 Exceptional   Rarely fails to meet class. Begins and ends class promptly to ensure for maximum instruction time. Conducts class for entire scheduled time. Adheres strictly to college's policy on attendance and records absences daily. Willingly accepts teaching assignments and responsibilities as scheduled.

4 Very Good   Almost always meets class for full time period. Arrives early to class to ensure that instruction can begin on time. Encourages attendance throughout the quarter and records daily attendance. Willingly accepts teaching assignments as scheduled.

3 Acceptable   Usually meets classes. Reminds students of attendance policy. Records daily attendance. Accepts teaching assignments as scheduled.

2 Marginal   Occasionally fails to meet class. Dismisses students early from class. Explains attendance requirements at beginning of quarter. Fails to keep daily attendance, but has a general idea of who misses class. Usually accepts teaching assignments.

1 Unacceptable   Occasionally fails to meet class without notifying students. Fails to begin and end classes promptly. Does not encourage or record daily attendance. Accepts teaching assignments after a confrontation.

2. **Methods of Instruction/Content Knowledge** - Presents lectures, demonstrations, or provides laboratory supervision using appropriate methods of instruction and resources. Provides out-of-class assistance when necessary.

5 Exceptional   Uses a variety of methods, aids, and resource people as part of presentations. Identifies objectives clearly and teaches to fulfill the objectives. Demonstrates mastery and comprehensive knowledge in subject area. Encourages student involvement. Stimulates and maintains student interest. Solicits students to investigate coursework outside of class.

4 Very Good   Uses a variety of methods and aids to increase students' interest. Teaches to specific objectives thereby wisely using class time. Exhibits conceptual knowledge in subject area. Presents materials which enhance instruction and student learning. Involves students in presentations. Assists students outside of class when needed.

3 Acceptable   Varies method of presentation to increase student interest. Establishes class objectives. Demonstrates knowledge of subject. Encourages student participation. Encourages students to seek additional help outside of class.

2 Marginal   Generally uses same method of presentation. Occasionally loses sight of objectives during class time. Demonstrates knowledge in subject area. Presents essential information. Answers student questions, but fails to involve students in presentations. Is available for outside help when needed.

1 Unacceptable   Strays from subject matter during classes. Exhibits minimal knowledge of subject matter. Discourages student participation. Unavailable to students seeking help outside of class.

3. **Presentation of Instruction** - Provides formalized verbal instruction to students.

5 Exceptional   Demonstrates exceptional verbal communications with students. Gains students' attention quickly. Usually presentations are both captivating and highly informative. Instructional style is praised by students and is conducive to student learning.

4 Very Good   Demonstrates excellent classroom presence. Communicates using a wide range of verbal skills which greatly enhance the learning environment. Students look forward to his/her classes. Students respond to instructional style gaining conceptual knowledge of material.

3 Acceptable   Presents information with adequate verbal skills. Maintains students' attention. Students gain essential information.

2 Marginal   Communicates information but fails to regularly maintain students' attention. Students gain essential information. Slow to adjust instructional style to needs of students.

1 Unacceptable   Presentations are less than adequate due to lack of preparation, confusion, poorly modulated voice, monotony, grammatical errors, distracting mannerisms, etc. Learning is an ordeal for students. Fails to monitor and adjust teaching style to encourage student attentiveness.

4. **Student Evaluation** - Provides opportunity for student evaluation of course and instructor, reviews evaluations, and utilizes results.

5 Exceptional   Serves as a resource person or exhibits leadership in developing or refining evaluation procedures. Attends workshops and conducts research related to student evaluations of instructors. In addition to the administration's quarterly evaluations, administers alternative forms of evaluations for more personal and specific feedback. Thoroughly reviews strengths and weaknesses as viewed by students.

4 Very Good   Assists administration in developing adequate evaluation procedures. Administers evaluations according to established procedures. Reviews results and takes steps to incorporate recommendations in future instructional endeavors so to minimize any weaknesses and capitalize on the strengths.

3 Acceptable   Administers student evaluations according to established procedures. Reviews results and uses feedback to improve teaching.

2 Marginal   Generally follows established procedures in process of evaluation. Fails to utilize the results of students' responses.

1 Unacceptable Fails to follow established procedures for students to evaluate course or instructor.

5. **Pre and Post Clinical Conferences (Nursing)** - Conducts pre and post conferences to prepare students for clinical experiences and to evaluate the day's activities.

5 Exceptional   Assumes the role of a group leader in conducting pre and post conferences. Uses creative strategies for gaining students' attention. Promotes an understanding of important concepts. Demonstrates exceptional ability to inspire creative thinking among students. Expectations include a sophisticated level of active student participation. Facilitates students to integrate subject matter knowledge and theory into practical application. Students look forward to conferences and eagerly participate.

4 Very Good   Implements objective of the day by encouraging students' suggestions as to how the objective could be achieved. Makes an effort to involve all students. Uses post conference to follow through with the objective in practice. Maintains flexible format to include unforeseen situations that may occur.

3 Acceptable   Conducts pre and post conferences in a non-threatening, student-oriented atmosphere. Uses objective of the day to relate theory to practice and suggests possibilities of application to students. Elicits student input. Uses post conference to follow up on concepts introduced during the pre conference.

2 Marginal   Conducts pre conferences using a lecture format. Gives assignments and objective for the day. Elicits minimal student input and offers little discussion of how to meet the objective. Post conferences recount activities rather than tie experiences to objective.

1 Unacceptable Conducts brief and/or incomplete pre and post conferences. Makes assignments for the day with no discussion of how objective might be met. Atmosphere is teacher-directed with no student input or direction of how to meet the objective.

6. **Clinical Instruction (Nursing)** - Supervises and instructs students in clinical facility.

5 Exceptional Demonstrates substantial expertise in clinical area. Demonstrates an up-to-date comprehensive knowledge base of clients' medical regimens. Manages own time wisely by organizing the environment and situations for the benefit of both students and clients. Skillfully challenges students' higher order thinking skills and promotes an atmosphere of inquiry. Meticulously monitors students' activities with clients by clarifying, verifying, and amplifying students' assessment of the situation.

4 Very Good Demonstrates expertise in clinical area. Is up-to-date on clients' conditions at all times and knows clients' medical care plans. Efficiently organizes self and students to meet clients' needs and students' objectives. Maintains careful balance between eliciting responses from students and giving direct answers when necessary. Carefully monitors students' activities with clients. Verifies students' assessments of clients and assists students in clarifying and refining their skills.

3 Acceptable Demonstrates overall competence in clinical area. Knows clients' diagnoses and treatment regimens. Organizes self and students to meet the needs of clients within the clinical facility. Encourages students' to discover answers on own, but provides answers if necessary. Supervises students' activities with clients. Observes all invasive procedures and medications.

2 Marginal Exhibits basic knowledge in clinical area. Is aware of clients' diagnoses and treatment regimens. Ineffectively organizes students in meeting clients' needs. Directly instructs students rather than eliciting their ideas. Casually supervises students' activities with clients.

1 Unacceptable Exhibits deficiencies in clinical knowledge. Is minimally aware of clients' diagnoses and treatment regimens. Is very disorganized, finding it difficult to supervise students and meet clients' needs. Inhibits students' thinking for themselves. Provides little supervision of students' activities with clients.

C. Testing/Evaluation

1. **Evaluation Development and Administration** - Develops and administers tests or other methods for measuring student achievement, and informs students of evaluation procedures and criteria.

    5 Exceptional   Develops tests or other procedures that utilize different item forms or data collection efforts which not only are congruent with the instructions being evaluated but which also tap students' strengths. Attends workshops aimed at improving evaluation methods. Elicits and considers students' input regarding evaluation format. Conducts reliability and validity studies of evaluation procedures.

    4 Very Good   Carefully weighs different measures to ensure that evaluation data gathered is congruent with course objectives. Provides comfortable conditions for evaluations. Allows adequate time for test completion or assignments. Ensures that evaluation procedures are reliable and valid.

    3 Acceptable   Uses a variety of methods besides tests for assessing student achievement/performance. Uses statistical methods of analysis when appropriate. Discusses methods of evaluation with students.

    2 Marginal   Develops and uses tests to measure students' achievement/performance. Informs students of procedures to be used.

    1 Unacceptable   Utilizes subjective methods insufficient to assess students' achievement/performance. Fails to inform students about evaluation procedures.

2. **Feedback to Students** - Provides results and critiques tests and other evaluations, records scores and corrections.

    5 Exceptional   Provides immediate feedback to students by reviewing tests or performance during class following administration. Grades and returns evaluations the next class day. Provides explanatory comments (on evaluation) to clarify answer. Critiques test in class, adjusts scores when appropriate. Allows students opportunities to defend their answers or opinions if appropriate. Provides information from test analysis to students.

    4 Very Good   Usually returns evaluations/assignments by the next class session. Explains scoring procedure. Reviews all items, adjusting for errors in scoring. Informs students of the range of scores and the appropriate descriptive statistics.

3 Acceptable   Usually returns tests/assignments within one week. Answers any student questions. Does not review every item. Clarifies areas of confusion and reteaches if necessary.

2 Marginal   Returns evaluation results before next evaluation with little explanation of scores and no critique. Allows students with questions to come by office or stay after class. Records scores.

1 Unacceptable   Feedback from evaluations is delayed. Fails to provide evaluation results before next evaluation. Neglects to regularly inform students of their progress during the course.

3. **Final Exams and Grades** - Files copies of examinations with Dean. Following exam schedule, computes final course grades and submits grades to Registrar.

5 Exceptional   Always administers final exams according to schedule. Consistently files copy of all exams with Dean of Instruction before designated time. Computes final course grades and files these with the Registrar before designated time. Submits grade sheets and attendance reports for classes.

4 Very Good   Administers final exams according to schedule. Files on time copies of all exams with Dean of Instruction. After grading exams, computes final course grades and submits appropriate documents to Registrar before designated time.

3 Acceptable   Administers final exams usually adhering to schedule. Files copies of all exams with the Dean of Instruction. Submits course grades to Registrar by designated time.

2 Marginal   Administers final exams, other than during exam schedule. Fails to file copies of exams on time with the Dean of Instruction. Usually submits course grades to Registrar on time.

1 Unacceptable   Administers little, if any, final evaluation procedure. Usually submits final course grades to Registrar late.

4. **Pre and Post Clinical Conferences (Emergency Medical Technician-EMT)** - Conducts pre and post clinical conferences to determine value of clinical experiences to students and assesses student progress.

5 Exceptional   Effectively uses clinical conferences as a way to know each student personally. Provides an atmosphere of professionalism. Is available for discussing clinical issues at times other than regular conference hours. Encourages students' self-appraisal of their clinical performance. Uses clinical evaluations as a medium to build on students' strengths and concentrate on reducing any deficiencies.

4 Very Good   Makes an effort to hold pre and post conferences in an atmosphere of supportive learning rather than evaluation. Maintains a flexible format in conferences in order to accommodate for any unforeseen situations that may occur. Actively assists students in discovering how to improve their decision-making skills.

3 Acceptable   Conducts necessary pre and post conferences. Encourages student input, offers support, gives advice, and redemonstrates skills when necessary. Thoroughly explains and follows through on clinical objectives. Demonstrates an acute interest in students' perceptions of clinical experiences. Accepts suggestions for improvement.

2 Marginal   Conducts pre and post conferences as necessary to evaluate previous clinical experiences. Uses conferences to make assignments. Allows student feedback regarding their experiences.

1 Unacceptable   Uses pre and post conferences chiefly for assignment purposes. Meets with students infrequently. Limits student input. Fails to critically evaluate feedback or consider alternate action.

D. Student Affairs

1. **Advising** - Assists students in course selection and career planning. Refers students to proper resources for personal counseling.

5 Exceptional   Guides students to discover their own career goals and directions. Refers students to knowledgeable persons in area of career interest. Exhibits concern for students with personal problems and refers them for personal counseling. Contacts advisees who fail to attend sessions with faculty advisor.

4 Very Good   Maintains communication with counselors regarding possible programs to meet students' career or personal needs. Exhibits genuine professional interest in individual students and their mental health. Maintains confidentiality in all counseling matters. Keeps advisees informed of all commitments to program.

3 Acceptable   Uses planned student program of study provided by the counselor to help advisee plan quarterly and/or yearly schedules. Exhibits knowledge of college and community resources for personal counseling and refers students appropriately.

2 Marginal   Agrees to serve as student advisor when requested. Assists students in course selections. Is difficult for students to locate faculty member.

1 Unacceptable Fails to work with students on course selections. Recommends that students seek help elsewhere. Is generally unavailable to students for career planning.

2. **Extracurricular Activities** - Serves as a club sponsor for student organizations and participates in special campus activities.

5 Exceptional   Surveys student population to determine interests or needs not being met. Initiates and/or sponsors new school-wide activities and events. Organizes new student groups, publicizing and encouraging participation. Actively participates in extracurricular activities or events.

4 Very Good   Sponsors or takes leadership role in a student club or organization. Engages in extracurricular activities or events as club sponsor. Encourages faculty and student participation in campus-wide events.

3 Acceptable   Sponsors events that involve students and faculty. Participates in campus-wide extracurricular activities or events.

2 Marginal   Attends special campus-wide events occasionally. Assists with club or organization; if necessary, provides minimal leadership.

1 Unacceptable Exhibits little interest in or information about student activities. Rarely attends special events. Fails to assist student organizations.

3. **Job Placement** - Writes letters of recommendation and otherwise assisting in job placement as requested.

5 Exceptional   Promptly writes letters of recommendation matching students' knowledge, skills, and abilities against requirements of particular jobs. Uses a wide variety of possible sources of career information. Calls and makes periodic visits to prospective employers to locate job opportunities.

4 Very Good   Writes letters of recommendation, taking into account students' abilities. Uses various sources of career information. Continuously updates job announcements. Relays pertinent information to appropriate personnel.

3 Acceptable   Writes letters of recommendation upon request.   Posts job announcements and makes oral announcements to groups of students in related fields where applicable.

2 Marginal   Writes requested letters of recommendation after some delay. Posts job announcements where applicable.

1 Unacceptable   Refuses to write letters of recommendation for students.   Lacks knowledge about area job opportunities.

E. Administration

1. **Personal Office Schedule** - Maintains office hours and posts and adheres to personal schedule.

5 Exceptional   Develops and posts a meticulous schedule.   Adheres to time and duties specified on schedule.   Posts whereabouts if not able to meet schedule.   Always is prompt for classes and appointments. Routinely works on campus more than the 35 hours per week minimum.

4 Very Good   Develops and posts a detailed schedule.   Usually follows schedule as posted.   Meets classes and appointments on time.   Works 35 hours or more per week on campus.

3 Acceptable   Posts schedule as required.   Usually follows schedule and can be located when needed.   Meets classes on time.   Maintains 35 hours on campus per week minimum.

2 Marginal   Post schedule which denotes general rather than specific duties in blocks of time.   Generally adheres to schedule.   Is sometimes late for class.   Usually maintains a minimum of 35 hours on campus per week.

1 Unacceptable   Fails to post hours and/or schedule.   Difficult to locate during office hours.   Arrives for class late.   Works less than the 35 hours on campus per week minimum.

2. **Administrative Responsibilities** - Performs administrative support tasks and carries out official policies.

5 Exceptional   Handles administrative responsibilities in an exemplary manner. Exceeds required or expected administrative performance standards.   Analyzes data from reports and makes recommendations Assists in the development of policies.   Contributes to the development of reports, forms, records, and other materials.

4 Very Good   Consistently performs administrative responsibilities in a professional manner. Makes special effort always to comply with official polices. Carefully checks reports and other requested materials for accuracy and usually submits them early.

3 Acceptable   Performs administrative responsibilities. Complies with official policies. Prepares accurate reports and other requested materials and submits them on time.

2 Marginal   Usually performs requested administrative responsibilities. Generally complies with official policies. Submits reports and other requested materials occasionally late or improperly prepared.

1 Unacceptable   Neglects to perform required administrative responsibilities. Acts contrary to official policies. Submits late or poorly prepared reports and other requested materials.

3. **Supply Economy** - Conserves expendable supplies and accounts for and takes care of equipment.

5 Exceptional   Continuously practices supply economy. Maintains accurate inventory control records of assigned equipment. Reads technical/operator manuals and arranges for preventive maintenance. Immediately attends to requests and follows up on needed repairs. Considers needs of others in using item of equipment. Always follows proper checkout and return procedures for equipment.

4 Very Good   Makes special effort to economize on supplies. Maintains inventory control records of assigned equipment. Promptly arranges for repairs and maintenance. Ensures that proper checkout and return procedures are followed.

3 Acceptable   Conserves supplies. Accounts for items of equipment. Reports needed repairs and maintenance. Follows proper checkout and return procedures.

2 Marginal   Generally conserves supplies. Can usually locate items of equipment. Fails to be knowledgeable about necessary repairs and maintenance schedules. Normally follows proper checkout and return procedures.

1 Unacceptable   Wastes supplies. Is unaccountable for loses or damages in equipment. Neglects to follow proper checkout and return procedures.

4. **Interpersonal Communications** - Communicates and interfaces with colleagues and administration both on a one-on-one basis, in faculty committees, and in other group settings.

> *5 Exceptional*   Assumes proactive leadership role in all types of situations by providing innovative solutions and inspiration to others. Carries out and follows up on assignments. Resolves conflicts even in stressful situations. Is highly regarded and influential among colleagues.

> *4 Very Good*   Assumes leadership role with individuals and groups. Attempts to resolve problems amicably. Carries out assignments promptly. Establishes effective and productive relationships with colleagues.

> *3 Acceptable*   Works effectively with individuals and groups. Attends necessary meetings. Offers suggestions to problems. Willingly accepts and carries out special assignments. Assumes collegial role.

> *2 Marginal*   Usually works with individuals and attends meetings. Accepts and carries out special assignments when required. Conflicts with colleagues are rare.

> *1 Unacceptable* Refuses to work with individuals. Absent from required meetings. Refuses assignments. Is occasionally indifferent, antagonistic, or disruptive. Conflict with colleagues occur.

F. Professional Development

1. **Independent Self-Improvement** - Keeps informed of new information relating to subject area, including better teaching methods and techniques.

> *5 Exceptional*   Maintains professional membership(s) and may hold a leadership position within a professional organization. Reads and researches information from professional journals. Initiates research projects in area of specialty. Holds appropriate terminal degree. Pursues academic work beyond the terminal degree.

> *4 Very Good*   Maintains membership(s) in a professional organization. Seeks new sources of information and uses resources of organization to enrich knowledge of subject matter or techniques of instruction. Confers with faculty members in other schools, universities, or research institutions. Progresses toward attaining appropriate terminal degree.

3 Acceptable   Seeks information in subject areas and keeps updated on latest developments in subject area or in related field. Holds appropriate master's degree in current subject area. Makes progress toward one year of advanced study in subject area.

2 Marginal   Reads material available through college in subject areas and in field of education. Holds appropriate master's degree in subject area of instruction.

1 Unacceptable   Does little or no independent reading in subject area or teaching methods. Makes little or no progress toward eliminating noted deficiencies in subject area or in teaching methods and techniques.

2. **Classes and Workshops** - Participates in programs, workshops, and classes to maintain credentials and competencies in subject area.

5 Exceptional   Organizes and/or leads special in-service programs or workshops in subject area. Stimulates interest in new area for possible study which addresses an identified need.

4 Very Good   Prepares and/or presents a segment of a workshop or program in subject area. Maintains professional credentials.

3 Acceptable   Attends and actively participates in programs, workshops, and classes designed for maintaining credentials and competencies.

2 Marginal   Participates in only those classes or programs mandatory for maintaining credentials.

1 Unacceptable   Refrains from participating in in-service programs, workshops, or advanced study to maintain credentials and competencies in subject area.

G. Community Service

1. **Extension** - Serves as a resource person in area of expertise for community organizations, businesses, or special events.

5 Exceptional   Provides major leadership for public service activities, community businesses, and organization upon request. Advises area businesses of possible services. Actively serves on organizational boards for special events or programs. Takes responsibility for special events in area of expertise. Analyzes area needs for possible new programs or events. Submits informative and timely news releases regarding relevant educational information and opportunities.

4 Very Good   Promotes and carries out public service activities. Serves on organizational boards for special events or programs. Submits informative and timely new releases regarding relevant educational information and opportunities. Provides education to the public by writing newspaper articles on subjects of general interest and submitting them for approval.

3 Acceptable   Carries out public service activities. Makes formal presentation in area of expertise to local clubs and organizations when requested. Provides information to media when appropriate to publicize programs or special events.

2 Marginal   Will usually attend community programs and share information in area of expertise. Submits necessary information to media when requested.

1 Unacceptable Avoids participation in public service or extension programs. Neglects to provide information to media when appropriate.

2. **Community Relations** - Represents the institution and contributes to the welfare of the community through participation in civic affairs.

5 Exceptional   Projects an extremely positive image of the institution. Serves in a leadership capacity in several different areas of community life. May serve as chairperson for special events. Acts as stimulus for new ideas for improving quality of community life.

4 Very Good   Is an asset to the institution. Maintains interest in several aspects of community life, taking a leadership role in at least one.

3 Acceptable   Positively represents the institution. Attends some community events, providing a supportive role in special area of interest. Carries out responsibilities when asked.

2 Marginal   Is not particularly identified with the institution. Attends some community events.

1 Unacceptable Projects a negative image of the institution. Exhibits little or no interest or involvement in community activities.

3. **Continuing Education Instruction** - Teaches continuing education classes, keeps special groups updated on Emergency Medical Technician (EMT) standards, and teaches skills and competencies to health professionals.

> *5 Exceptional*   Works with area health professionals to develop new courses or revise old ones. Works on regional, state, or national committees to evaluate current teaching requirements and maintenance of credentials. Develops and teaches innovative and state-of-the-art material in classes. Communicates latest EMT standards.

> *4 Very Good*   Writes letters, sends out brochures, or otherwise communicates with former students, clinical units, and college administration to keep them apprised of current EMT standards. Develops and teaches up-to-date information in classes.

> *3 Acceptable*   Plans and teaches classes for health professionals to keep them proficient in EMT skills and competencies, in addition to teaching the required classes.

> *2 Marginal*   Teaches the required minimum hours of continuing education classes in order to maintain EMT credentials.

> *1 Unacceptable*   Teaches less than the minimum number of hours of continuing education classes to maintain EMT credentials.

PERFORMANCE
APPRAISAL FORM

Southern Union State Junior College

PART I   IDENTIFICATION

Name _____

Position __Library Technician_____

Rating Period From _____ To _____

Rater Name _____

Rater Title _____

Department _____

Date Employed _____

Rating Scale Key

1 Fails to Meet Job Requirements
2 Essentially Meets Job Requirements
3 Fully Meets Job Requirements
4 Meets Job Requirements with Distinction
5 Exceeds Job Requirements

PART II   RATING SCALES FOR MAJOR RESPONSIBILITIES

A. Physical Processing	PCT. 35%	RATING:	1 ☐	2 ☐	3 ☐	4 ☐	5 ☐
Creating and maintaining records, and correctly performing related tasks needed to facilitate locating and obtaining library materials.		COMMENTS					

B. Circulation	PCT. 20%	RATING:	1 ☐	2 ☐	3 ☐	4 ☐	5 ☐
Carrying out prescribed procedures, and accurately maintaining records regarding the borrowing of books and other materials by library users.		COMMENTS					

C. Acquisition	PCT. 15%	RATING:	1 ☐	2 ☐	3 ☐	4 ☐	5 ☐
Ordering and receiving books, periodicals, and other materials; and accurately maintaining records.		COMMENTS					

D. Reference	PCT. 10%	RATING:	1 ☐	2 ☐	3 ☐	4 ☐	5 ☐
Assisting library users by providing information services, answering questions, assisting in locating library materials, and integrating information into cataloging system.		COMMENTS					

E. Cataloging and Classification	PCT. 10%	RATING:	1 ☐	2 ☐	3 ☐	4 ☐	5 ☐
Accurately compiling information and properly entering classifications of library materials, and integrating information into cataloging system.		COMMENTS					

F. General and Administrative	PCT. 10%	RATING:	1 ☐	2 ☐	3 ☐	4 ☐	5 ☐
Carrying out administrative support services and activities in accordance with institution policies and procedures.		COMMENTS					

G.	PCT. %	RATING:	1 ☐	2 ☐	3 ☐	4 ☐	5 ☐
		COMMENTS					

PART III   RATING SCALES FOR MAJOR RESPONSIBILITIES

A. INSTRUCTIONAL PLANNING AND PREPARATION	(10%)	Rating 1 2 3 4 5
1. Course Development 2. Instructional Preparation 3. Clinical Preparation (Nursing) 4. Clinical Planning (EMT)		☐ ☐ ☐ ☐ ☐
Comments		

B. INSTRUCTION	(50%)	Rating 1 2 3 4 5
1. Schedule and Attendance 2. Method of Instruction 3. Presentation of Instruction 4. Student Evaluation 5. Pre and Post Clinical Conferences (Nursing) 6. Clinical Instruction (Nursing)		☐ ☐ ☐ ☐ ☐
Comments		

C. TESTING/EVALUATION	(10%)	Rating 1 2 3 4 5
1. Evaluation Development and Administration 2. Feedback to Students 3. Final Exams and Grades 4. Pre and Post Clinical Conferences (EMT)		☐ ☐ ☐ ☐ ☐
Comments		

D. STUDENT AFFAIRS	(10%)	Rating 1 2 3 4 5
1. Advising 2. Extracurricular Activities 3. Job Placement		☐ ☐ ☐ ☐ ☐
Comments		

E. ADMINISTRATION (10%)	Rating
	1 2 3 4 5
1. Personal Office Schedule 2. Administrative Responsibilities 3. Supply Economy 4. Interpersonal Communications	☐ ☐ ☐ ☐ ☐
Comments	

F. PROFESSIONAL DEVELOPMENT (5%)	Rating
	1 2 3 4 5
1. Independant Self-Improvement 2. Classes and Workshops	☐ ☐ ☐ ☐ ☐
Comments	

G. COMMUNITY SERVICE (5%)	Rating
	1 2 3 4 5
1. Extension 2. Community Relations 3. Continuing Education Instruction (EMT)	☐ ☐ ☐ ☐ ☐
Comments	

PART IV   OBJECTIVES

ACHIEVEMENT OF PERSONAL AND PROFESSIONAL (INCLUDING DIVISIONAL) OBJECTIVES

OBJECTIVES NEXT REVIEW PERIOD

PART V PERFORMANCE DISCUSSION AND SUMMARY

DESCRIBE THE FACULTY MEMBER'S STRONG POINTS

DESCRIBE ANY AREAS OF WEAKNESS

DESCRIBE ANY SPECIFIC ACTIONS NEEDED TO IMPROVE PERFORMANCE

SUMMARIZE OVERALL PERFORMANCE AS DETERMINED IN YOUR JOINT DISCUSSION

ART VI SIGNATURES

This report is based on my observation and knowledge of both the faculty member and the job.

My signature indicates that I have reviewed this appraisal. It does not mean that I agree with the results.

_____
Division Chair   Date

_____
Dean of Instruction   Date

_____
Faculty Member   Date

Exhibit 5

Exhibit 5 is a set of behavioral observation scales for the same faculty position. In this case the individual is observed and rated on a five-point Likert-type scale as to the frequency of the observed behavior. In completing the appraisal, the department head circles 1 if the individual has engaged in the behavior 0-64 percent of the time, 2 if 65-74 percent, 3 if 75-84 percent, 4 if 85-94 percent, and 5 if 95-100 percent. A total score is determined by summing the responses to all behavioral items.

Behavioral Observation Scale (BOS) for Appraising Faculty

A. Performance Dimension of *Instructional Planning and Preparation*

Assumes a leadership role in divisional planning meetings and other aspects of curriculum development.

Almost Never   1   2   3   4   5   Almost Always

Shares responsibilities in divisional planning meetings regarding course development.

Almost Never   1   2   3   4   5   Almost Always

Makes valid suggestions regarding course offerings and/or modifications of current offerings.

Almost Never   1   2   3   4   5   Almost Always

Serves as a resource person in specialty area to colleagues.

Almost Never   1   2   3   4   5   Almost Always

Updates and submits course outlines (syllabi) on time to Dean's office.

Almost Never   1   2   3   4   5   Almost Always

Suggests way to improve current course/program offerings.

Almost Never   1   2   3   4   5   Almost Always

Selects and uses textbooks that currently reflect the latest technology and practices in the field.

Almost Never   1   2   3   4   5   Almost Always

Develops, maintains, and previews additional resources, such as films or tapes for reference, timing, and quality.

Almost Never   1   2   3   4   5   Almost Always

Utilizes a variety of teaching methods and aids.

Almost Never   1   2   3   4   5   Almost Always

Develops outlines and notes which cover the key concepts of the course objectives.

Almost Never   1   2   3   4   5   Almost Always

Presentations are implemented emphasizing key concepts.

Almost Never   1   2   3   4   5   Almost Always

Comprehensively integrates lecture, etc. with textbook and/or other relevant curricular materials.

Almost Never   1   2   3   4   5   Almost Always

Lectures are planned to promote inquiry and decision-making skills among students in order to solve problems.

Almost Never   1   2   3   4   5   Almost Always

Instructional times is optimally planned for benefit of students.

Almost Never   1   2   3   4   5   Almost Always

Arrives for class prepared with necessary materials for classroom instruction.

Almost Never   1   2   3   4   5   Almost Always

Meets regularly with clinical staff or head nurse.

Almost Never   1   2   3   4   5   Almost Always

Interactions with facility staff reflects a mutual respect and appreciation of the clinical facility and nursing program.

Almost Never   1   2   3   4   5   Almost Always

Implements strategies to improve and facilitate optimal clinical experiences for students.

Almost Never   1   2   3   4   5   Almost Always

Critically assesses students' progress with the clinical program.

Almost Never   1   2   3   4   5   Almost Always

Arranges and modifies clinical experiences in order to ensure that students' needs are being met.

Almost Never   1   2   3   4   5   Almost Always

Possesses indepth knowledge of the facility's system.

Almost Never   1   2   3   4   5   Almost Always

Follows facility's routine, procedures, and regulations in clinical programs.

Almost Never   1   2   3   4   5   Almost Always

Acts as a facilitator to clinical staff in updating plans for clinical experiences.

Almost Never   1   2   3   4   5   Almost Always

Conducts meetings with supervisors in clinical facility to plan assignments, experiences, and schedules in order to promote students' overall development and attainment of course objectives.

Almost Never   1   2   3   4   5   Almost Always

Monitors student progress throughout the quarter by encouraging feedback from supervisors on students' performances and experiences.

Almost Never   1   2   3   4   5   Almost Always

Modifies experiences or assignments of students as deemed necessary.

Almost Never   1   2   3   4   5   Almost Always

Promotes and actively works toward maintaining a program that ensures students of positive clinical experiences.

Almost Never   1   2   3   4   5   Almost Always

Assesses how clinical experiences and assignments are meeting students' needs.

Almost Never   1   2   3   4   5   Almost Always

Acknowledges input from students as a possible way to improve clinical experiences.

Almost Never   1   2   3   4   5   Almost Always

Total _____

◆   ◆   ◆   ◆   ◆

B. Performance Dimension of *Instruction*

Meets class as scheduled.

Almost Never   1   2   3   4   5   Almost Always

Conducts class for full time period as scheduled.

Almost Never   1   2   3   4   5   Almost Always

Encourages attendance throughout the quarter.

Almost Never   1   2   3   4   5   Almost Always

Records daily attendance.

Almost Never   1   2   3   4   5   Almost Always

Accepts teaching assignments willingly as scheduled.

Almost Never   1   2   3   4   5   Almost Always

Notifies students in advance if class will be cancelled.

Almost Never   1   2   3   4   5   Almost Always

Makes alternate arrangements if class is not to meet.

Almost Never   1   2   3   4   5   Almost Always

Uses a variety of methods, aids, and resource people as part of presentations.

Almost Never   1   2   3   4   5   Almost Always

Establishes and teaches to clearly identified objectives.

Almost Never   1   2   3   4   5   Almost Always

Demonstrates mastery and comprehensive knowledge in subject area.

Almost Never   1   2   3   4   5   Almost Always

Encourages student involvement and participation.

Almost Never   1   2   3   4   5   Almost Always

Stimulates and maintains student interest.

Almost Never   1   2   3   4   5   Almost Always

Involves students in presentations.

Almost Never   1   2   3   4   5   Almost Always

Assists students outside of class.

Almost Never   1   2   3   4   5   Almost Always

Lectures are presented at an appropriate volume, tone, and rate of speech.

Almost Never   1   2   3   4   5   Almost Always

Demonstrates exceptional verbal communications/rapport with students.

Almost Never   1   2   3   4   5   Almost Always

Gains students' attention within the first five minutes of class.

Almost Never   1   2   3   4   5   Almost Always

Instructional style is praised by students.

Almost Never   1   2   3   4   5   Almost Always

When needed, modifies instructional style in order to maintain students' attention.

Almost Never   1   2   3   4   5   Almost Always

Students gain essential information.

Almost Never   1   2   3   4   5   Almost Always

Assists administration in developing adequate student evaluation procedures.

Almost Never   1   2   3   4   5   Almost Always

Serves as a resource person or exhibits leadership in developing or refining student evaluation procedures.

Almost Never   1   2   3   4   5   Almost Always

Attends workshops and conducts research in the area of student evaluations of faculty.

Almost Never   1   2   3   4   5   Almost Always

Administers student evaluations according to established procedures.

Almost Never   1   2   3   4   5   Almost Always

Reviews results and uses student feedback to improve teaching.

Almost Never   1   2   3   4   5   Almost Always

Administers alternative forms of student evaluations, in addition to the administration's quarterly evaluations in order to achieve more personal and specific feedback from students regarding course and faculty performance.

Almost Never   1   2   3   4   5   Almost Always

Conducts pre and post conferences in a non-threatening student-oriented atmosphere.

Almost Never   1   2   3   4   5   Almost Always

Uses objective of the day to relate theory to practice.

Almost Never   1   2   3   4   5   Almost Always

Facilitates students' learning by integrating subject matter knowledge and theory in practical application.

Almost Never   1   2   3   4   5   Almost Always

Elicits student input regarding clinical experiences and analysis of the day's activities.

Almost Never   1   2   3   4   5   Almost Always

When necessary, suggests possible clinical applications to students.

Almost Never   1   2   3   4   5   Almost Always

Uses post conferences to follow up on concepts introduced during the pre conference.

Almost Never   1   2   3   4   5   Almost Always

Assumes the role of a group leader in conducting pre and post conferences.

Almost Never   1   2   3   4   5   Almost Always

Maintains a flexible format in conferences in order to address unforeseen situations that may occur.

> Almost Never   1   2   3   4   5   Almost Always

Expectations include a sophisticated level of active student participation.

> Almost Never   1   2   3   4   5   Almost Always

Demonstrates expertise in clinical area.

> Almost Never   1   2   3   4   5   Almost Always

Uses constructive time management techniques.

> Almost Never   1   2   3   4   5   Almost Always

Demonstrates an up-to-date comprehensive knowledge base of clients' medical regimens.

> Almost Never   1   2   3   4   5   Almost Always

Organizes the clinical environment to maximize efficient/effective service delivery.

> Almost Never   1   2   3   4   5   Almost Always

Establishes an atmosphere of higher-order inquiry among students.

> Almost Never   1   2   3   4   5   Almost Always

Monitors/supervises students' activities with clients by clarifying, verifying, and amplifying students' assessments of the clinical situation.

> Almost Never   1   2   3   4   5   Almost Always

Encourages students' to discover answers on own, but provides answers if necessary.

> Almost Never   1   2   3   4   5   Almost Always

Observes all invasive procedures and medications.

> Almost Never   1   2   3   4   5   Almost Always

Total _____

♦   ♦   ♦   ♦   ♦

C. Performance Dimension of *Testing/Evaluation*

Uses a variety of methods besides tests for assessing student achievement/performance.

| Almost Never | 1 | 2 | 3 | 4 | 5 | Almost Always |

Attends workshops to learn state-of-the-art in test and measurement techniques.

| Almost Never | 1 | 2 | 3 | 4 | 5 | Almost Always |

Elicits and considers students' input regarding evaluation format.

| Almost Never | 1 | 2 | 3 | 4 | 5 | Almost Always |

Assigns weights to assessment measures congruent with course objectives.

| Almost Never | 1 | 2 | 3 | 4 | 5 | Almost Always |

Allows adequate time for test completion or assignments.

| Almost Never | 1 | 2 | 3 | 4 | 5 | Almost Always |

Provides appropriate physical environment/conditions for evaluations.

| Almost Never | 1 | 2 | 3 | 4 | 5 | Almost Always |

Conducts reliability and validity studies of evaluation procedures.

| Almost Never | 1 | 2 | 3 | 4 | 5 | Almost Always |

Uses statistical methods of analysis in evaluations.

| Almost Never | 1 | 2 | 3 | 4 | 5 | Almost Always |

Discusses methods of evaluation with students.

| Almost Never | 1 | 2 | 3 | 4 | 5 | Almost Always |

Returns students' tests/assignments within one week.

| Almost Never | 1 | 2 | 3 | 4 | 5 | Almost Always |

Provides explanatory comments (on evaluation) to clarify appropriate response.

| Almost Never | 1 | 2 | 3 | 4 | 5 | Almost Always |

Critiques tests in class.

    Almost Never   1   2   3   4   5   Almost Always

Answers student questions regarding evaluations.

    Almost Never   1   2   3   4   5   Almost Always

Adjusts test scores to reflect actual credit earned when appropriate .

    Almost Never   1   2   3   4   5   Almost Always

Allows students opportunities to defend their answers or opinions.

    Almost Never   1   2   3   4   5   Almost Always

Explains scoring procedures for evaluations.

    Almost Never   1   2   3   4   5   Almost Always

Informs students of the range of scores and the appropriate descriptive analysis.

    Almost Never   1   2   3   4   5   Almost Always

Provides clarification of test items which students question.

    Almost Never   1   2   3   4   5   Almost Always

Administers final exams according to schedule.

    Almost Never   1   2   3   4   5   Almost Always

Files copies of all exams with the Dean of Instruction.

    Almost Never   1   2   3   4   5   Almost Always

Submits course grades to Registrar by designated time.

    Almost Never   1   2   3   4   5   Almost Always

Conducts pre and post conferences in a professional atmosphere.

    Almost Never   1   2   3   4   5   Almost Always

Is available to discuss clinical issues at times other than at regular conference hours.

    Almost Never   1   2   3   4   5   Almost Always

Encourages students' self-appraisal of their clinical performance.

Almost Never   1   2   3   4   5   Almost Always

Uses clinical evaluations as a medium to build on students' strengths while concentrating on reducing any deficiencies.

Almost Never   1   2   3   4   5   Almost Always

Assists students in learning techniques to improve their clinical decision-making skills.

Almost Never   1   2   3   4   5   Almost Always

Encourages student input, offers support, gives advice, and redemonstrates skills when necessary to promote students' progress.

Almost Never   1   2   3   4   5   Almost Always

Explains and follows through on clinical experiences.

Almost Never   1   2   3   4   5   Almost Always

Accepts suggestions for improving clinical experiences.

Almost Never   1   2   3   4   5   Almost Always

Provides an atmosphere of supportive learning rather than evaluation.

Almost Never   1   2   3   4   5   Almost Always

Accommodates for any unforeseen situations by conducting conferences within a flexible format.

Almost Never   1   2   3   4   5   Almost Always

Conducts clinical conferences to promote personal student-faculty relationships.

Almost Never   1   2   3   4   5   Almost Always

Total _____

◆   ◆   ◆   ◆   ◆

D. Performance Dimension of *Student Affairs*

Guides/counsels students to discover their own career goals and directions.

    Almost Never   1   2   3   4   5   Almost Always

Maintains communications with counselors regarding possible programs to meet students' career or personal needs.

    Almost Never   1   2   3   4   5   Almost Always

Uses planned student program of study provided by the counselor to help advise plan quarterly or yearly schedules.

    Almost Never   1   2   3   4   5   Almost Always

Agrees to serve as student advisor as requested.

    Almost Never   1   2   3   4   5   Almost Always

Refers students to knowledgeable persons in area of career interest.

    Almost Never   1   2   3   4   5   Almost Always

Demonstrates a professional interest in students' mental health.

    Almost Never   1   2   3   4   5   Almost Always

Refers students for personal counseling when counseling is warranted.

    Almost Never   1   2   3   4   5   Almost Always

Maintains confidentiality in all counseling matters.

    Almost Never   1   2   3   4   5   Almost Always

Exhibits knowledge of college and community resources for personal counseling.

    Almost Never   1   2   3   4   5   Almost Always

Continuously informs advisees of responsibilities and commitments to program.

    Almost Never   1   2   3   4   5   Almost Always

Assumes a leadership role in a student club or organization.

    Almost Never   1   2   3   4   5   Almost Always

Sponsors extracurricular events that involve students and faculty.

Almost Never   1   2   3   4   5   Almost Always

Participates in campus-wide extracurricular activities or events.

Almost Never   1   2   3   4   5   Almost Always

Actively encourages faculty and student participation in campus-wide events.

Almost Never   1   2   3   4   5   Almost Always

Identifies student interests and needs not currently addressed in extracurricular activities.

Almost Never   1   2   3   4   5   Almost Always

Initiates new school-wide programs or organizes new student groups that further meet the interests and needs of the student population.

Almost Never   1   2   3   4   5   Almost Always

Writes letter of recommendation matching students' knowledge, skills, and abilities against requirements of a particular job.

Almost Never   1   2   3   4   5   Almost Always

Uses various sources of career information to locate job opportunities.

Almost Never   1   2   3   4   5   Almost Always

Calls and visits prospective employers to identify potential new job opportunities.

Almost Never   1   2   3   4   5   Almost Always

Routinely updates and immediately posts job announcements.

Almost Never   1   2   3   4   5   Almost Always

Informs students of job opportunities in their field of endeavor.

Almost Never   1   2   3   4   5   Almost Always

Total _____

◆ ◆ ◆ ◆ ◆

E. Performance Dimension of *Administration*

Develops and posts detailed schedule.

    Almost Never   1   2   3   4   5   Almost Always

Adheres to schedules as posted.

    Almost Never   1   2   3   4   5   Almost Always

Posts whereabouts if not in office during scheduled office hours.

    Almost Never   1   2   3   4   5   Almost Always

Meets classes and schedules at designated time.

    Almost Never   1   2   3   4   5   Almost Always

Routinely works on campus more than the 35 hours per week minimum.

    Almost Never   1   2   3   4   5   Almost Always

Consistently performs administrative responsibilities in a professional manner.

    Almost Never   1   2   3   4   5   Almost Always

Exceeds required or expected administrative performance standards.

    Almost Never   1   2   3   4   5   Almost Always

Prepares accurate reports and other requested materials as requested.

    Almost Never   1   2   3   4   5   Almost Always

Submits reports on time and completes other administrative support tasks as scheduled.

    Almost Never   1   2   3   4   5   Almost Always

Complies with official policies.

    Almost Never   1   2   3   4   5   Almost Always

Analyzes data from reports and makes recommendations.

    Almost Never   1   2   3   4   5   Almost Always

Assists in the development of official policies, reports, forms, etc.

Almost Never   1   2   3   4   5   Almost Always

Continually practices supply economy.

Almost Never   1   2   3   4   5   Almost Always

Notifies appropriate authority when certain expendable supplies are low.

Almost Never   1   2   3   4   5   Almost Always

Maintains accurate inventory control records of assigned equipment.

Almost Never   1   2   3   4   5   Almost Always

Follows proper checkout and return procedures for equipment.

Almost Never   1   2   3   4   5   Almost Always

Follows preventative maintenance schedules for equipment.

Almost Never   1   2   3   4   5   Almost Always

Reports and immediately arranges for repairs and maintenance.

Almost Never   1   2   3   4   5   Almost Always

Assumes a proactive leadership role in situations by providing innovative solutions to problems.

Almost Never   1   2   3   4   5   Almost Always

Is viewed as a facilitator by colleagues and other administrators.

Almost Never   1   2   3   4   5   Almost Always

Maintains a professional and productive relationship with colleagues.

Almost Never   1   2   3   4   5   Almost Always

Attempts to resolve conflicts amicably among individuals and groups.

Almost Never   1   2   3   4   5   Almost Always

Promptly performs and follows up on assignments and commitments.

Almost Never   1   2   3   4   5   Almost Always

Attends necessary meetings.

Almost Never   1   2   3   4   5   Almost Always

Total _____

◆   ◆   ◆   ◆   ◆

F.   Performance Dimension of *Professional Development*

Maintains membership(s) in a professional organization in area of specialization.

Almost Never   1   2   3   4   5   Almost Always

Holds a leadership position within a professional organization in area of specialization.

Almost Never   1   2   3   4   5   Almost Always

Reads and incorporates research from professional journals in academic work.

Almost Never   1   2   3   4   5   Almost Always

Initiates research projects in specialty area.

Almost Never   1   2   3   4   5   Almost Always

Uses resources of organization to enrich personal knowledge of subject matter or related techniques.

Almost Never   1   2   3   4   5   Almost Always

Pursues advanced academic coursework beyond current academic degree.

Almost Never   1   2   3   4   5   Almost Always

Maintains notarity in their field among colleagues on campus, at other institutions, and within the state.

Almost Never   1   2   3   4   5   Almost Always

Organizes and leads special in-service programs or workshops in subject area.

Almost Never   1   2   3   4   5   Almost Always

Assumes a leadership role in preparing/presenting a segment of a workshop or in-service program.

| Almost Never | 1 | 2 | 3 | 4 | 5 | Almost Always |

Maintains professional credentials.

| Almost Never | 1 | 2 | 3 | 4 | 5 | Almost Always |

Attends and actually participates in programs, workshops, and classes designed for maintaining credentials and competencies.

| Almost Never | 1 | 2 | 3 | 4 | 5 | Almost Always |

Total _____

◆　◆　◆　◆　◆

G. Performance Dimension of *Community Service*

Provides major leadership for public service activities, community businesses, and organizations upon request.

| Almost Never | 1 | 2 | 3 | 4 | 5 | Almost Always |

Performs public service activities through formal presentations to local clubs and organizations in area of expertise.

| Almost Never | 1 | 2 | 3 | 4 | 5 | Almost Always |

Actively serves on organizational boards for special events or programs.

| Almost Never | 1 | 2 | 3 | 4 | 5 | Almost Always |

Analyzes community needs for possible new programs or events.

| Almost Never | 1 | 2 | 3 | 4 | 5 | Almost Always |

Submits informative and timely news releases publicizing educational information, activities, and opportunities.

| Almost Never | 1 | 2 | 3 | 4 | 5 | Almost Always |

Projects an extremely positive image of the institution within the community.

| Almost Never | 1 | 2 | 3 | 4 | 5 | Almost Always |

Contributes to the welfare of the community by participating in civic affairs.

Almost Never   1   2   3   4   5   Almost Always

Takes a leadership role in at least one civic organization.

Almost Never   1   2   3   4   5   Almost Always

Acts as a stimulus for new ideas to promote the welfare of the community.

Almost Never   1   2   3   4   5   Almost Always

Works with area health professionals to develop new courses or revise old ones in the area of continuing education.

Almost Never   1   2   3   4   5   Almost Always

Works on regional, state, or national committees to evaluate current teaching requirements and maintenance of credentials.

Almost Never   1   2   3   4   5   Almost Always

Teaches innovative, state-of-the-art information in continuing education classes.

Almost Never   1   2   3   4   5   Almost Always

Communicates the latest Emergency Medical Technician (EMT) standards to various health professional groups, former students, clinical units, and college administrators.

Almost Never   1   2   3   4   5   Almost Always

Total _____

Performance Dimensions for *Appraising Faculty*	Totals
A. Instructional Planning and Preparation	_____
B. Instruction	_____
C. Testing/Evaluation	_____
D. Student Affairs	_____
E. Administration	_____
F. Professional Development	_____
G. Community Service	_____
Overall Faculty Performance Total	_____

Appendix B: Checklist for Legal Requirements*

This appendix addresses the major considerations involved in validating a performance appraisal system using a content validity strategy. It is in the form of a checklist for meeting minimum legal requirements. It is not a comprehensive guide to conducting in-depth or quantitative studies.

*The Checklist for Legal Requirements was developed by James A. Buford, Jr. and Bettye B. Burkhalter, Auburn University, AL 36849.

Checklist for Legal Requirements

Requirements	Authority	How Addressed
Determine if content validity strategy is appropriated.	"Uniform Guidelines," Sec 14 (C) (1)	A content validity strategy is appropriate for procedures designed to measure observable work behavior(s) or work product(s).
Avoid procedures based on traits or constructs such as "intelligence, aptitude, personality, common sense, judgement, leadership and spatial ability."	Uniform Guidelines, Sec 14 (C) (1) *Wade v. Mississippi Cooperative Extension Service*, 372 F. Supp. 126 (1974), 7EPD 9186	No direct measurement of traits or constructs should be built into the system. A trait may, however, be inherent in a job related behavior or outcome.
"There should be a job analysis which includes an analysis of important work behavior(s) required for successful job performance and their relative importance and if the behavior results in a work product analysis of the work product(s)"	"Uniform Guidelines," Sec 14 (C)(2)*Greenspan v. Automobile Club of Michigan*, 22 FEP 195 (1980) *Albermarle Paper Co. v. Moody*, U.S. Supreme Court Nos. 74-389 and 74-128, 10 FEP Cases 1181, 1975	Job analysis should be conducted for each job. Relative importance of job domains, or task areas, should be established during job analysis. Frequency and criticality of tasks should be established during job analysis.
"A (performance appraisal) procedure designed to measure work behavior may be developed specifically from the job or job analysis in question...."	"Uniform Guidelines." Sec 14 (C) (3)	Domains indentified in job analysis can be defined in terms of acceptable level of job performance. *or* Tasks or duties which are similar can be grouped together to form criterion areas.

Checklist for Legal Requirements (continued)

Requirements	Authority	How Addressed
"To demonstrate content validity, a user should show that the behaviors demonstrated in the (performance appraisal) procedures are representative of behavior(s)...work product(s) of the job."	"Uniform Guidelines," Sec 14 (C) (4)	Performance criteria should developed for critical and important duties in each domain and weighted in accordance with the overall importance of the domain.
"The manner and setting of the (performance appraisal) procedure should closely approximated the work situation."	"Uniform Guidelines," Sec 14 (C) (4)	Performance criteria should be described in terms of actual job conditions.
The performance appraisal process should be administered under controlled and standardized conditions.	*Brito v. Zia Company*, 478 F. 2d. 1200 (1973)	A performance appraisal instrument should be developed. The instrument should facilitate the rating process and be keyed to both the criteria and method. Provisions should be made for weighting the ratings according to the rules of combination. Indentification, comments, and signatory sections should be included.
A report or memorandum of how the system was developed should be prepared.	*Vulcan Pioneers, Inc. v. New Jersey Department of Civil Service*, 588 F. Supp. 732 (D.C.N.J. 1984) "Uniform Guidelines," Sec 15 (C)(1-9)	A content validity report should be prepared. This report should include as a minimum: user(s), location(s), and date(s); job analysis - content of the job; performance appraisal procedure and its content; relationship between performance appraisal procedure and the job; alternative procedures investigated; uses and applications; contact person; accuracy and completeness.

Developed by James A. Buford, Jr. and Bettye B. Burkhalter (1988), Auburn, University, Alabama 36849.

74437

Bettye B. Burkhalter is Professor in the College of Education and Director of the Auburn University Economic Development Institute. She teaches Personnel Administration courses at the graduate level and has had extensive experience in private business and in industrial and governmental affairs. She received Ed.D. and Ph.D. degrees from The University of Alabama and was selected for the the Loreé Research Award for her Ph.D. research in the area of Human Resource Management (HRM). Dr. Burkhalter has consulted widely with both public and industrial organizations in the area of performance appraisal.

James A. Buford, Jr. is Adjunct Professor in the College of Business and Management Scientist and Coordinator of Management Development, Cooperative Extension Service, Auburn University. He received a Ph.D. degree from The University of Georgia and is accredited by the Personnel Accreditation Institute. He has taught, conducted research, and consulted widely in the area of performance appraisal. Dr. Buford has designed legally defensible performance appraisal systems in both the public and private sectors.

Following are the affiliations of the other contributors appearing in *Performance Appraisal: Concepts and Techniques for Postsecondary Education.*

Richard J. Federinko is President of Southern Union State Junior College which enrolls 2,500 students at its three campuses. He received his Ph.D. degree in Higher Education Administration from Florida State University.

Mark E. Meadows is Professor and Head, Counseling and Counseling Psychology Department, in the Auburn University College of Education. He received his Ed.D. in Counseling and Student Personnel from The University of Georgia.

Edith A. Miller is an Associate Professor in the Department of Educational Foundations, Leadership, and Technology at Auburn University. She received her Ed.D. degree in Educational Psychology from The University of Georgia.

William I. Sauser, Jr. is Associate Vice President for Extension and Professor at Auburn University. He received his Ph.D. in Industrial/Organizational Psychology from the Georgia Institute of Technology.